Have Your Say ③

Have Your Say  3

Listening and Speaking Skills and Practice

Frank Bieri

Niagara College

Alex MacGregor

Niagara College

OXFORD

UNIVERSITY PRESS

OXFORD
UNIVERSITY PRESS

Oxford University Press is a department of the University of Oxford.
It furthers the University's objective of excellence in research, scholarship,
and education by publishing worldwide. Oxford is a registered trade mark of
Oxford University Press in the UK and in certain other countries.

Published in Canada by
Oxford University Press
8 Sampson Mews, Suite 204,
Don Mills, Ontario M3C 0H5 Canada

www.oupcanada.com

Library and Archives Canada Cataloguing in Publication
Bieri, Frank, author
Have your say 3 : listening and speaking skills and practice / Frank
Bieri and Alex MacGregor.

Accompanied by an audio CD.
ISBN 978-0-19-901788-1 (paperback)

1. English language–Textbooks for second language learners.
2. English language–Study and teaching (Higher)–Foreign speakers.
3. English language–Spoken English–Problems, exercises, etc.
I. MacGregor, Alex, author   II. Title.

PE1128.B54 2016   428.3'4   C2015-906743-X

Cover image: Rawpixel/Shutterstock

Oxford University Press is committed to our environment.
This book is printed on Forest Stewardship Council® certified paper
and comes from responsible sources.

Printed and bound in the United States of America

1 2 3 4 — 19 18 17 16

For Shirley and Bob who always showed the spirit, beauty, and power of communication, and Yumiko for standing with me.

For Ruedi, an inspiration for perseverance and following your dreams. Thank you also to Colleen, Eden, and Alec because without your ongoing encouragement and support this would not have been possible.

SCOPE AND SEQUENCE CHART

CHAPTER	LISTENING	
	Listening Selections	Listening and Note-Taking Strategies
(1) THE IMPACT OF ENGLISH	1. Al Jazeera Panel Discussion—Global English 2. British Council Panel Discussion—Who Cares about English?	• Identifying a speaker's intent • Previewing questions before listening to build context • Focusing on ideas rather than words • Using a chart to connect notes to speakers • Identifying varying points of view
(2) COMMUNICATION TECHNOLOGY	1. CBC Interview—Internet Linguistics 2. CBC Narrative—Living in Two Worlds	• Making a pre-listening plan • Making a personal connection to what you hear in order to remember details more easily • Using symbols, short forms, and abbreviations • Organizing a narrative chronologically
(3) HUMANS AND TECHNOLOGY	1. CBC Interview—Surveillance Society 2. CBC Interview—Getting Good Gadgets	• Recognizing bias • Prioritizing ideas • Focusing on questions • Building a visual system
(4) OUR RELATIONSHIP WITH NATURE	1. CBC Interview—Fish Swimming in Pharmaceutical Soup 2. PBS News Hour Report—Can a City Produce Zero Waste?	• Listening for cause and effect • Recognizing transitions and sequencing • Organizing by cause and effect • Organizing by introduction, body, conclusion
(5) THE INFLUENCE OF THE MEDIA	1. McGill University Round-Table Discussion—Hurdles to Ensuring Human Rights 2. CBC Interview—Meet Anne Marie Owens	• Visualizing mind maps • Anticipating answers and questions • Developing a mind map for a panel discussion • Preparing a notes chart for interviews

	SPEAKING		
	Communicative Focus and Speaking Strategies	**Grammar**	**PRONUNCIATION**
	• Describing by classifying • Describing problems and suggesting solutions • Being concise to keep the listener's attention	• Describing with adjective clauses and participial adjectives • Matching verb tenses with the time of the context	• Recognizing and using voiced sounds • Pronouncing consonants (-s endings) • Pronouncing consonants (-ed endings) • Pronouncing vowel sounds
	• Asking questions to gather information • Summarizing information • Paraphrasing information • Expressing an analysis • Rephrasing to facilitate communication • Organizing an analysis for presentation	• Using interrogatives • Using reported speech	• Reducing vowel sounds • Recognizing syllables • Applying syllable stress
	• Making inferences • Using discourse markers • Supporting a proposition with infographics • Stating opinions	• Modals	• Recognizing thought groups • Applying thought group stress
	• Giving instructions and explaining procedures • Expressing obligation • Managing a discussion • Developing a proposal • Making a presentation • Using sequencing words • Identifying with listeners	• Using the imperative • Using articles correctly	• Linking words within thought groups • Deleting sounds in words
	• Beginning a group presentation • Participating in a panel discussion • Moderating a panel discussion • Explaining complex ideas • Building social networks • Maintaining a neutral position • Using anecdotes to add a personal touch	• Expressing degrees of certainty • Using the subjunctive mood	• Applying common contractions • Applying fast speech strategies

SCOPE AND SEQUENCE CHART (*continued*)

CHAPTER	LISTENING	
	Listening Selections	Listening and Note-Taking Strategies
⑥ SOCIAL CHANGE	1. The Lost Lectures—Sarah Corbett: A Craftivist Story 2. The Congress of the Humanities and Social Sciences Lecture—Don Tapscott: Macrowikinomics: Social Sciences and Social Change in the Age of Social Media	• Understanding meaning by recognizing emphasis • Asking critical questions while listening, to stay engaged and focused • Using organizational cues • Recognizing emphatic strategies
⑦ YOUNG PEOPLE AND THE BUSINESS WORLD	1. Cornell University Lecture—Ralph Christy: Why Small is Still Beautiful 2. CBC Debate—Interns: To Pay or Not to Pay	• Asking reflective questions • Avoiding bias • Pausing and reflecting • Organizing by speaker
⑧ TRANSITIONING TO PROFESSIONAL LIFE	1. CBC Interview—The New Resumé 2. McGill University Interview—Social Networking and Your Electronic Footprint	• Recognizing lists of examples or steps buried in a speaker's speech • Visualizing what the speaker is saying • Organizing by contrasting • Organizing by pros and cons

SPEAKING		
Communicative Focus and Speaking Strategies	**Grammar**	**PRONUNCIATION**
• Synthesizing content from multiple sources • Using rhetorical language • Managing a seminar • Opening a discussion by briefly paraphrasing or summarizing information • Controlling tone • Adding depth to discussions by asking deeper-level questions	• Reporting speech—questions and commands	• Using common intonation patterns—Part 1
• Evaluating arguments • Debating—presenting arguments • Debating—presenting counter-arguments • Familiarizing oneself with contextual vocabulary	• Using emphatic structures • Using noun clauses as embedded questions	• Using common intonation patterns—Part 2
• Preparing for a job interview • Arguing persuasively • Negotiating • Promoting yourself • Speaking persuasively	• Applying the passive voice	• Projecting and speaking clearly • Pausing for effect

Contents

CHAPTER 3

HUMANS AND TECHNOLOGY   63

CHAPTER 4

OUR RELATIONSHIP WITH NATURE   93

CHAPTER 7

YOUNG PEOPLE AND THE BUSINESS WORLD   175

CHAPTER 8

TRANSITIONING TO PROFESSIONAL LIFE   205

AUTHOR ACKNOWLEDGEMENTS

Thank you to all who dedicate their time to learning a new language. You have provided ideas and contexts for making language learning fun and interesting.

We would like to thank the amazing team at Niagara College International for their willingness to put the student language experience first, and making the field of language teaching an adventure.

We would also like to thank Carolyn Pisani at Oxford University Press Canada for all of the hours she put in reviewing and editing this work. Her efforts were invaluable.

REVIEWERS

Oxford University Press would like to express appreciation to the instructors and coordinators who graciously offered feedback on *Have Your Say 3* at various stages of the developmental process. Their feedback was instrumental in helping to shape and refine the series.

Patricia Birch	Brandon University	John Iveson	Sheridan College
Margaret Chell Gregory	Université de Montréal	Susan McElwain	Mohawk College
		Patrice Palmer	Mohawk College
Heather Cordeiro	Mohawk College	Donna Sharpe	Mount Allison University
Shelagh Cox	Mount Royal University	Mary Tang	Centennial College
Joan Dundas	Brock University	Tony Vernon	Camosun College
Steve Gates	Mount Allison University		

INTRODUCTION

Overview

Audience

Have Your Say 3: Listening and Speaking Skills and Practice is an integrated listening and speaking text for advanced learners of English in Intensive English, EAP, and post-secondary academic preparation programs. It is designed to take learners from intermediate ability to comprehend and use language to an advanced level, with a focus on listening and producing authentic language in authentic contexts. *Have Your Say 3* is the third book in a three-level course in listening and speaking.

Approach

Have Your Say 3 is a higher-level version of the widely used Canadian text *Have Your Say 2: Listening and Speaking Skills and Practice*, and includes the same popular features. As with the intermediate text, *Have Your Say 3* is based on the concept that **learner-centredness** and exposure to authentic English and meaningful language in collaborative activities are motivating and provide a means for developing proficiency in listening and speaking. The approach of this advanced level text is grounded in three principles: **critical thinking**, which is vital in academic and social settings and enhances language skills; **reflection**, in which self-analysis leads to refinement of one's practices; and **activation**, the application of knowledge and skills to fluent usage.

Features of the Text

Listening Sections

Each chapter has two main listening sections. The selection of authentic audio and video files is from a variety of Canadian and international sources; each listening selection sets a conceptual theme for the lesson. Learners are invited to engage in activities focusing on social, technological, environmental, professional, and academic issues relevant to their lives in a modern knowledge-based society. The tasks that accompany the listenings afford learners opportunities to build a repertoire of cognitive and organizational academic listening skills.

Pre-Listening Activities

Prior to listening, learners exercise the opportunity to infuse their own life experiences and personal input into topic-based tasks. They also preview and practise manipulating lexical items through familiar, meaningful tasks to build retention and retrieval skills.

The lexical items listed in **Upfront Vocabulary** are integral to understanding each listening selection, but are not necessarily common words and phrases language learners at this level would study. In many cases they are jargon. Definitions of these often content-specific words, names of people and organizations, and abbreviations are provided up front to help learners access the issues and concepts of the lessons.

Note-Taking Skill Development and Practice

An important part of academic study is keeping a record of what was said during listening, so that key information can later be accessed for review. There are many reasons for speakers to share information and for listeners to listen. Each note-taking section in this book aims at teaching and giving opportunities to practise a variety of different strategies tailored to the purpose and audience of each type of authentic listening.

Listening Activities

These tasks and activities are designed to teach learners how to identify main ideas, recognize the details that support the speakers' ideas, and acknowledge speaker intent. In the Listening activities, students demonstrate their understanding and contemplate what they have heard.

Personalizing

Information becomes more interesting and memorable when a correlation can be made to learners' prior knowledge and understanding. Personalizing activities at the end of each listening section guide learners to make connections to the content of what they heard and to their own values and experiences.

Speaking Sections

Advanced learners require extensive practice in applying what they are learning. It is easy for students to focus too much on content and not enough on practical application. Speaking activities are most meaningful and memorable for learners when they build on students' knowledge of the world and of the language by adding new layers of communication in manageable chunks. *Have Your Say 3* does just that; it provides learners with many different types of speaking activities that incorporate real-life scenarios in language-learning contexts closely linked to the listenings and the overall theme of each chapter. Speaking activities are tied in with the vocabulary learned in the listening and provide opportunity for students to apply the skills and strategies of the Communication Focus sections. Equal importance is paid to oral and aural communication skills.

Communication Focus

Academic students use critical thinking skills to solve problems—it is the foundation of upper-level study. The Communication Focus sections correspond to the critical-thinking process, helping students systemize the way they organize and express their thoughts as they inquire, describe, classify, organize, analyze, hypothesize, summarize, evaluate, and argue.

Speaking Activities

The activities support the Communication Focus sections and learners' activation of new language, skills, and refinement of previously learned ones in contexts such as impromptu speeches, dialogues, discussions, seminars, and negotiations.

Grammar Notes

The grammatical component is based on the practices of application and reflection. When pertinent to the structures and expressions mentioned in the Communication Focus sections, grammar points are introduced and briefly explained. The emphasis is on facilitating correct self-expression and enhancing awareness of accuracy in speaking. To achieve this goal, learners are encouraged to reflect on their patterns of errors and practise correct forms in a wide variety of activities.

Listening and Speaking Strategies

A mixture of different learning strategies to aid in the development of listening and speaking skills appear in the margins throughout the chapters. These Listening and Speaking Strategies are carefully selected to support the Communication Focus of the chapter and provide jumping-off points for further explanation. Teachers may discuss the strategies learners can use and encourage them to try to use the new strategies to progress in their own communication outside of the classroom context.

Pronunciation Sections

The Pronunciation sections each have one or more focuses that are based on building awareness of the relationship of accuracy to understanding in varied upper-level speaking contexts, and of learners' own ability to pre-empt and correct errors resulting from bad habits. The Pronunciation Focus sections support student progress, from review of vowel and consonant sounds and the features of syllables, to prosodic elements of thought groups, by providing abundant opportunity for practice and application of the features taught and heard.

Communicating in the Real World

Language learning becomes most meaningful when students are able to apply what they have learned and practised in class to real-life situations beyond the classroom. Each chapter has a final section that helps students make a connection between what they have learned in the clinical and safe learning environment that is the classroom and applying the communication focuses, pronunciation, grammar, and vocabulary in much less predictable authentic communication. One key aspect of these real-life applications is the sharing of experiences with the class in order to reflect and grow as language users.

Self-Evaluation

At the end of each chapter students are provided with a self-evaluation chart that they are encouraged to use. This practice is consistent with the underlying principles of activation and reflection. Learners benefit from taking ownership of their learning, recording what they have done, and planning what they need to do next. It is an important step towards independence when learners can first ask themselves if they have met their goals and then, if necessary, develop a plan for further practice.

CHAPTER 1

The Impact of English

Describing by classifying

Describing problems and suggesting solutions

THINKING AND TALKING

Work with a partner to brainstorm the factors that have influenced your English language learning and list your ideas. Your list may include general reasons why you study English: people who influenced you, advice you have been given, or study environments, or may be more specific and personal.

LISTENING 1

Before You Listen

PRE-LISTENING ACTIVITY 1

Would you call yourself a successful learner of English? Why? A good command of English has led to success for many people, but to gain that command one may encounter difficulties. Drawing from your own experience, discuss with your group what you have found to be the difficulties of learning a second language.

PRE-LISTENING ACTIVITY 2

With your group, consider the question "Is the English language actually destroying the world's diversity rather than uniting it?" Begin a discussion about how English could threaten cultural identities or mother tongues of other countries. Start by sharing examples of English words and phrases that have entered into your own language with your group and then by expressing your observations about the effect of English words being used in your own language.

UPFRONT VOCABULARY

Globish	compound of the words *global* + *English*
mother tongue	the language that you first learn to speak when you are a child
Hinglish	compound of *Hindi* + *English*
colonist	a person who settles in a country that is ruled by a more powerful one
imperialism	the fact of a powerful country increasing its influence over other countries through war, business, culture, etc.*
dominant	more important, powerful, or noticeable than other things*
lingua franca	a shared language of communication used between people whose main languages are different*
multilingual	speaking or using several different languages*

*Definition courtesy of *Oxford Advanced Learner's Dictionary*.

PRE-LISTENING VOCABULARY

A. You will hear the following words in the Al Jazeera discussion "Global English". Work with a partner to match the vocabulary with their definitions.

Vocabulary	Definitions
linguistic	_____diversity_____ range of many people or things that are very different from each other*
denounce	_____ fixed firmly into a solid object or substance*
nuance	_____ to make a country or an institution more democratic*
democratize	_____ to enter (or make somebody enter) a place or an organization secretly*
concession	_____ more important, powerful, or noticeable than other things*
deplore	_____ connected with language or the scientific study of language
~~diversity~~	_____ to strongly criticize somebody/something that you think is wrong, illegal, etc.
infiltrate	_____ a very slight difference in meaning, sound, colour, or somebody's feelings that is not usually very obvious*
dominant	_____ to strongly disapprove of something and criticize it, especially publicly
embedded	_____ something that you allow or do (or allow somebody to have), in order to end an argument or to make a situation less difficult*

*Definition courtesy of *Oxford Advanced Learner's Dictionary.*

B. Fill in the blanks using the vocabulary from the chart.

1. Charlene and Maryssa _____ the treatment of the caged animals.

2. To _____ the country, the first step was allowing its citizens to vote.

3. The Canadian government had to _____ the actions of the rioters.

4. The shocking events of the past are _____ in his memory.

5. I enjoyed the book although I know I missed the cultural _____.

6. When buying a new car, Alex made no _____ to cost and bought a BMW.

7. In the animal kingdom, the female is often the _____ partner controlling most situations.

Listening STRATEGY

Good listeners are able to identify why a speaker is talking. A speaker's intent (to narrate, inform, or persuade) can be recognized by catching key verbs. If the listener understands the speaker's intent, he or she can anticipate the direction the speaker will take.

8. The extent of different cultures and languages is an indicator of Canada's _____.

9. Shauna speaks five languages fluently; her _____ ability is very high.

10. The spy was able to _____ the deepest areas of the government's security system.

PRE-LISTENING ACTIVITY 3

Discuss with a partner how each of the verbs in the list might be used and write them in the Speaker Intent chart below. When you are finished, check your answers with the whole class.

argue	entertain	clarify	tell
classify	investigate	compare	demonstrate
convince	move	criticize	present
define	prove	list	describe
state cause and effect		explain (a process)	

Speaker Intent			
Narrate	**Inform**		**Persuade**
tell	demonstrate		argue

Track 1

Imperialism is a country's expansion of power and land borders to control and influence other countries or territories through economic, cultural, military, linguistic, or other means. For example, the British Empire expanded over much of the world.

You will hear a panel discussion called "Speaking 'Globish': Is the Spread of English a Form of Linguistic Imperialism?" The moderator of this broadcast, Riz Khan, asks whether the worldwide spread of English is promoting global understanding or is simply linguistic imperialism, using a language to spread a nationalistic or cultural agenda. His panel guests, author Robert McCrum and linguist Robert Phillipson, discuss the impact of English and the **pros and cons** of the spread of English as a global language. You will hear the moderator and his two interviewees as well as questions from the show's listeners.

Note-Taking

Note-taking in chart form helps keep facts connected to the speakers who stated them. Look at the note-taking chart created for the panel discussion. Some sentences in the chart give a choice of terms. Listen to the complete discussion for the first time. It is long, so listen carefully for the information to complete the notes in the chart by circling the choices you hear. When you've finished, share your notes with a partner to discuss the similarities and differences between your notes.

Main Ideas in Question Form	Details from Answers and Comments
Q1. Moderator: What does the term *Globish* mean?	**McCrum:** A widespread/slightly **improved/overused/simplified** version of English.
Q2. Moderator: Wouldn't learning Globish have a **standardizing/democratizing/cultural** effect?	**Phillipson:** Yes, but while people need to understand diversity of types of English, they also need to express their own cultural IDs and needs.
Q3. (sent by email): How much power does a country have to stop the onslaught of English?	**McCrum: second languages/mother tongues/foreign tongues** are more powerful, because they are the essential tongue.
Q4. (sent by email): Technology is often very English-centric. Why do you think that is?	**Phillipson:** I don't think that's correct. It's not true that all **invention/programming/writing** is taking place in English.
Q5. (phone caller): [What do you think about the phenomenon of] more and more English words "creeping in" to languages and cultures?	**McCrum:** It's just the nature of language and it's comparatively **safe/unimportant/harmless**.
Q6. Moderator: How do you feel about the impact of the loss of a **country/language/culture** for a nation of people?	**Phillipson:** Languages in countries like Nigeria and Tanzania will be disappearing as time goes on, and that is a tragedy.

Listening for the Main Ideas

A. Read the four questions below.

B. Listen to selections from the discussion on Global English and use your notes in the chart above to help you answer the questions.

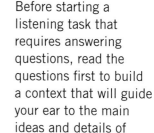 **Track 2**

1. How do the two experts feel about the worldwide spread of English? Does it promote understanding between people of different linguistic and cultural backgrounds, or does it only promote English culture?

   _____

   _____

   _____

   _____

Listening STRATEGY

Before starting a listening task that requires answering questions, read the questions first to build a context that will guide your ear to the main ideas and details of the listening.

2. An email questioner states: "Though the colonists are long gone, English has stayed and flourished." What is the reason the emailer thinks that the English language has flourished?

   _____

3. Why does linguist Dr. Phillipson disagree with the emailer's point of view regarding technology being English-centric?

_____

_____

4. How does author Robert McCrum feel about mixing English with other native languages so that new versions like Hinglish, Singaporean English, or Hong Kong English are evolving?

_____

Listening Comprehension

 Track 3

Listen to selections from the discussion on Global English once again and answer the questions as you listen. When you are finished, share your answers with a classmate and discuss any differences you may have.

1. Approximately how many native speakers of English are there in the world? _____

2. Approximately how many ESL learners are there in the world? _____

3. What was Robert McCrum's most recent accomplishment? _____

4. What is Dr. Robert Phillipson famous for? _____

5. Which country has made a strong effort to try to keep English out of its culture and language? _____

6. In what situations do people usually default to Globish? _____

Personalizing

Esperanto does not have the same evolution that every other language does. It is a language that was constructed (invented) in the early 19th century to foster international harmony. It was designed to be accessible—easy to learn. So, for the most part, people who learn Esperanto study it privately. The grammar is regular, and its vocabulary is largely made of prefixes, roots, and suffixes. Esperanto has not been recognized as a second language in any country, but has been adopted as the working language by some international organizations and agencies. There are many books published in Esperanto.

Can you imagine what these Esperanto sentences mean?

> **Studente anglan estas interesa.**

> **Mi loĝas en Kanado.**

With your group, discuss the question of language difficulty. Compared to your language, is English easier or more difficult to learn? Why? What are the features of English that are particularly difficult or confusing (for example, you may think that English spelling is not linked closely enough to pronunciation)?

Vocabulary and Language Chunks

Write the number of the expression next to its meaning. After checking your answers with your teacher or class, choose three expressions and make your own sentences.

Expressions	Meanings
1. cultural roots	_5_ hierarchy; used to determine the most and least important
2. draw a distinction	___ go to an automatic next step
3. default to something	___ the attributes of something
4. the nature of	___ background; heritage
5. pecking order	___ compare and contrast different things

SPEAKING 1

Communication Focus 1: Describing by Classifying

An early stage of the scientific process is to observe and describe. Following a system of classification makes descriptions more detailed and easier to understand.

Classifying Objects

Classifications	Examples
category	It's a kind/type of furniture.
shape	It's round/square/rectangular . . .
sense appeal	It smells/tastes/sounds/feels/looks . . .
material	It's made of wood/leather . . .
dimensions	It's two metres long . . .
parts	It has two main parts . . .
	It is attached to . . .
use	It's used to keep the rain off.
	It's used for warming the body.

Classifying What People Say

Classifications	Examples
description	Mother tongues are very powerful.

explanation	*Globish* is not my term; it was invented by a Frenchman, in fact.
persuasion	You need to change your behaviour.
definition	Liberalism is a political philosophy founded on the ideas of liberty and equality.
comparison	English is a common business language, as Latin was a thousand years ago.
process	Leaves lose chlorophyll, they turn red, and then they fall.
cause/effect	If everyone learned Globish, it would have a democratizing effect.
opinion	He writes that English is the language of ordinary people.

SPEAKING ACTIVITY 1

Take turns with your partner describing objects in your purse, bag, or pocket that your partner can't see. Describe them one at a time as specifically as you can until your partner has identified each one.

Examples:

It's usually tube-shaped.

It feels like wood, but it's soft.

It's a kind of bark.

Usually it's about 2.5 centimetres long and about half a centimetre in radius.

It's most often used to keep the wine in a wine bottle.

Answer: a cork

SPEAKING ACTIVITY 2

Divide into pairs for this guessing game based on Speaking Activity 1. You will use classifying and verbal clues only. Decide who will be Partner A, the first classifier. Partner B, close your book now.

Partner A: Tell your partner that he or she must try to guess the object after hearing some classification clues. You will reverse roles for the second half of the activity.

Classify the following objects in List A one at a time. Try not to use gestures.

After you and your partner have finished List A, close your book. Do not read B's items.

List A

chopsticks	a belt
a hand-held bell	a salt shaker
an umbrella	maple syrup

Partner B: Now it's your turn to classify the objects in List B for your partner, one at a time. Try not to use gestures.

List B

a computer mouse	a key
a battery	a suitcase
a dictionary	a bottle of hand sanitizer

SPEAKING ACTIVITY 3

Now work with your partner to classify abstract concepts such as bravery, friendship, satisfaction, peace, or your own concepts. Contrast the strategies you use to classify abstract concepts with the Communication Focus 1 strategies you used to classify concrete nouns like *umbrella* and *bottle* in Speaking Activities 1 and 2.

Grammar Note: Describing with Adjective Clauses and Participial Adjectives

Adjective clauses are used to describe. They begin with a pronoun (***that***, ***who***, ***which***) or an adverb (***when***, ***where***, ***why***).

> The phone <u>that I bought yesterday</u> fell into the pool.

> The studio <u>where David Crystal was interviewed</u> is in Toronto.

Active participial adjectives (adjectives with *–ing* endings) describe the **subject** of the sentence. They express the feeling or emotion that is being sent.

Examples:

The news excites Anna. (*news* is the subject)

The news is exciting. (active participial adjective)

The lecture motivated the listeners. (*lecture* is the subject)

The lecture was motivating. (active)

That question will interest the listeners. (*question* is the subject)

That question will be interesting. (active)

Passive participial adjectives (adjectives with *-ed* endings) describe the object of the sentence. They express the feeling that is being received.

Examples:

The news excites Sammy. (*Sammy* is the object)

Sammy is excited. (passive participial adjective)

The lecture motivated the listeners. (*listeners* is the object)

The listeners were motivated. (passive)

That information will interest the customers. (*customers* is the object)

The customers will be interested. (passive)

♙♙ SPEAKING ACTIVITY 4

Work in small groups and talk about famous people, places, times, inventors, and inventions from your country. Use sentences like:

> Canadarm, *which is used on the International Space Station*, was developed in the 1970s.
>
> Norman Bethune, *who worked alongside Mao Zedong in the Chinese Revolution*, was born in Gravenhurst, Ontario.
>
> Kingston, *where John A. Macdonald was born*, is the gateway to the Thousand Islands.
>
> The 1980s, *when neon colours were in fashion*, were a time of great social change.

♙♙ SPEAKING ACTIVITY 5

Take turns reading the sentences below and then saying them using both active and passive participial adjectives.

Example:

> Simon's attitude <u>troubles</u> Pierre.
>
> (active) Simon's attitude <u>is troubling</u> (for Pierre).
>
> (passive) Pierre <u>is troubled</u> (by Simon's attitude).

1. Learning a second language **interests** the students.
   (active)   Learning a second language is _____
   (passive) The students are _____

2. Language imperialism **worries** Dr. Phillipson.
   (active)   _____
   (passive) _____

3. John's accent **confused** Frieda.
   (active)   _____
   (passive) _____

4. The speaker's ideas about Globish **surprised** the listener.
   (active)   _____
   (passive) _____

♙♙ SPEAKING ACTIVITY 6

Take turns with your partner making sentences with the following adjectives.

surprising	surprised	encouraging	encouraged
motivating	motivated	embarrassing	embarrassed
amazing	amazed	disturbing	disturbed

👥 **SPEAKING ACTIVITY 7**

Work with your partner to create a dialogue with both passive and active participial adjectives. Use questions like these in your dialogue:

> **What surprises you?**
>
> **What excites you?**
>
> **Do you find . . . exciting?**
>
> **Do you think . . . is interesting?**
>
> **Don't you think . . . is annoying?**
>
> **Are you bothered by . . .?**
>
> **What frightens you the most?**

👥 **SPEAKING ACTIVITY 8**

Review the speech types listed in the Communication Focus, then work with a partner to classify what kind of speeches the following quotes are taken from. Circle the best answer. When you are finished, check your answers with the rest of the class and explain your choices.

1. "I started learning English because I didn't want to take chemistry class. Learning English seemed to have no benefit other than giving me big headaches and a lot of stress. However, now, I must admit that I thank the English language and my ability to use it for making me the person I am."

   comparison   persuasion   definition   process   cause/effect

2. "Inter-city rivalries exist around the world. For example, Beijing and Shanghai, Tokyo and Osaka, and Bogota and Medellin, to name a few. Montreal and Toronto are the best Canadian example of this phenomenon. While Toronto is a city of business, Montreal is a hub of culture and art. For many years Montreal was the most populated city in Canada, but in the 1960s the population of Toronto surpassed that of its Quebec rival . . ."

   comparison   persuasion   definition   process   cause/effect

3. "Cows produce raw milk on dairy farms all over the province. The milk is delivered to factories in tanker trucks where machines separate it into milk and cream. The milk is pasteurized at 72°C for 15 seconds, then cooled. Factory workers pack the milk into cartons, then into crates, and load the crates onto trucks. Finally, the pasteurized milk is delivered to local supermarkets where consumers buy it."

   comparison   persuasion   definition   process   cause/effect

👥 **SPEAKING ACTIVITY 9**

Choose one of the topics from the list and prepare a short impromptu speech on it to give to your group mates. Be careful in your speech to use only one of the two possible classifications. When you've finished, ask your group mates to classify your speech type.

Topics	Classification
exactly what I did this morning	description/process
how to make . . . (a national dish, e.g., kimchi)	process/opinion
why you should buy my cell phone	persuasion/description
why I chose my major	explanation/opinion
how I chose my major	explanation/process
my pet, my best friend	description/opinion

Grammar Note: Matching Verb Tenses with the Time of the Context

We use verb tenses to show time relationships clearly. One of the most common errors in speaking is the lack of consistency in tense usage. An effective communicator matches verb tenses with the time of the context.

Examples:

> **English today is very different from what it was in Shakespeare's time.**
> today: *is*   in the past: *was*

> **When Susan arrived, the lecture had already started.**
> when (at that time   previous to that time:
> in the past): *arrived*   *had (already) started*

> **I was thinking about you when you called.**
> continuous action (happening   when (at that time
> at that time): *was thinking*   in the past): *called*

> **Carolyn will have finished reading *War and Peace* by the time she graduates.**
> previous to that time   when (at that time
> (graduation): *will have finished*   in the future):
>   *graduates*

 SPEAKING ACTIVITY 10

Work with a partner to find what is wrong in the following questions and answers. Correct each sentence, and explain what mistakes were made.

Example:

Q: What will you do after class?

A: After class I go to a party.

Correction: After class I will go to a party.

Explanation: The question refers to the future tense, so the answer needs to do so too.

1. Q: Who borrowed my iPad?   A: Pat had borrowed it earlier this morning.

   _____
   _____

2. Q: Voulez-vous de l'aide?   A: Sorry, I'm not speaking French.

   _____
   _____

3. Q: What were you doing when the bell rang?   A: I got up and put my books in my bag.

   _____
   _____

4. Q: What pages have you read yesterday?   A: Huh?

   _____
   _____

5. Q: Are you ready?   A: Yeah, I'm having my books and notes.

   _____
   _____

6. Q: Did you see Steve at the party?   A: Yes, he had left just when I got there.

   _____
   _____

👥 SPEAKING ACTIVITY 11

Illustrate each sentence with a sketch. Then, discuss with your partner how the meaning changes from sentence a to sentence b because of the different verb tenses.

1. a. Yuki lived in Burnaby for a year. (simple past)
   b. Yuki has lived in Burnaby for a year. (present perfect)

2. a. Benedicte didn't finish her homework. (simple past)
   b. Benedicte hasn't finished her homework. (present perfect)

3. a. When Louisa arrived at the party, John left. (simple past)
   b. When Louisa arrived at the party, John had left. (past perfect)

4. a. Walter walks to school. (simple present)
   b. Walter is walking to school. (present continuous)

5. a. When Yaya arrived, Seong ate a sandwich. (simple past)
   b. When Yaya arrived, Seong was eating a sandwich. (past continuous)

LISTENING 2

Before You Listen

PRE-LISTENING ACTIVITY 1

The Quebec Board of the French Language (or *Office québécois de la langue française*) promotes and protects the French language in Canada. Its functions include processing complaints for non-respect of Quebec's language law, publishing dictionaries, and providing francization counselling. Discuss these questions with your group.

What do you think francization is?

What do you think governments or people should do to promote the French language in Quebec and in Canada?

What are they protecting the language from?

Does a language need to be protected?

PRE-LISTENING ACTIVITY 2

With your group, discuss the following question about dictionaries.

Should a dictionary clarify and describe the words of a language to determine what people *should say*, or should a dictionary be based on what people actually *do say*?

UPFRONT VOCABULARY

regulate	to control something by means of rules*
legislate	to make laws
descriptive	saying what somebody/something is like*
prescriptive	telling people what should be done*

*Definition courtesy of *Oxford Advanced Learner's Dictionary*.

PRE-LISTENING VOCABULARY

Use your dictionary to help you and your partner complete the sentences with these words from the audio.

ascertain	etymology	futile
self-regulating	replicate	derivatives

1. The word needs to be explained by its _____*etymology*_____ to see how it has changed over time.

2. The possibility of those changes being accepted is zero, so it's a _____ attempt.

3. They're trying to _____ a sports drink that already exists, not create a new one.

Listening STRATEGY

When listening, don't focus on syllables and understanding each word. This leads to too much time thinking about unknown vocabulary and can be frustrating. A strong listener focuses on what he or she does understand to link the pieces of what is understood and catch the single thought—the main idea—of each group of words.

4. Most new words are _____ of other words: they already exist in another form.

5. Franco's teammates helped the referee _____ who had scored the goal.

6. The study group is _____, so the participants don't require any supervision.

Note-Taking

The British Council is an organization that provides educational and cultural opportunities through its work in over 100 countries to help build and form education systems. At the British Council event recorded in this panel discussion, experts field questions from the audience.

 **Track 4**

Listen to the British Council panel discussion "Who Cares about English?" for the first time. Try not to concern yourself with who is talking, but focus on what is said and list the points of view expressed that you hear, in short phrases.

Topic: Regulating English
Sub-topic 1: Should it be regulated?
Speaker's point of view (POV): Regulating is a good thing, isn't it? (This is what you hear.) POV: **Regulating . . . good?** (This is what you write in your own words.)
POV:
POV:
POV:
POV:
Sub-topic 2: Adding new words to the English language
POV:
POV:
POV:
POV:
POV:
Sub-topic 3: Who should regulate English?
POV:
POV:
POV:

Listening for the Main Ideas

 Track 5   Listen to the panel discussion "Who Cares about English?" once again and answer the four questions.

1. Explain panel chair John Knagg's question, "(Regulating) is a good thing, isn't it?"
    a. He feels control of the language is unnecessary because everyone understands.
    b. He thinks control of the language is necessary so that everyone understands.

2. What questions are asked about English having a prescriptive language authority like French does?
    a. Who would decide the rules? What is France doing now?
    b. Do we need this in England? Who would run it?

3. What do the speakers agree is the strength of a language like English?
    a. It isn't regulated, it changes, and it grows.
    b. It is regulated, it uses many foreign words, and it is spoken around the world.

4. Why is choosing 12 "worthies" (knowledgeable people) to regulate the language futile?
    a. Other countries would never agree on what a British regulator decided.
    b. Twelve people would not represent all the countries where English is spoken.

Listening Comprehension

 Track 6   **A.** Read the questions below.

B. Listen to the panel discussion "Who Cares about English?" once again and answer the six questions.

1. According to the first panellist, what kind of people were the key historical legislators who organized and recorded the English language?

2. "The OED (*Oxford English Dictionary*) is the final word. It is descriptive." What does it describe?

3. Why is a word like *achybreaky* in the OED?

4. What is the name of the French authority the panel refers to?

5. When, according to the female panellist, is it unnecessary to create new words?

6. Finish this sentence: "English is self-regulating through _____, _____, and _____."

C. When you are finished, share your answers with a classmate and discuss any differences you found in your answers.

Personalizing

One of the panellists comments, "We have lots of different ways of saying one thing which provide different nuances." Consider what this statement means and discuss the following questions with a partner.

Does your vocabulary study include learning synonyms? If so, how do you learn synonyms and what exercises do you to do retain them?

Is there any value to learning words like *correct* and *identical* when you know the words *true* and *same*? Why not just learn one way to express certain concepts?

When you are finished, share your ideas with the class.

Vocabulary and Language Chunks

Note the usage of the following language chunks and then use each chunk to make a sentence of your own underneath the example given.

Language Chunks	Usage	Examples
make an impression on	used to describe when one produces a memorable effect on another person or thing	When Sharon's boyfriend arrived in a limousine to take her to the prom, it made quite an impression on her. _____ _____
the final word	used to refer to the last accepted statement on a topic	Sal has the final word on where we go when we head out for a drink. _____ _____
the tip of the iceberg	used to refer to superficial evidence (that can easily be seen) of a much larger issue (that remains hidden from the observer)	There are 500 French words in the OED, but French is just the tip of the iceberg because there are many more words from other languages. _____ _____

SPEAKING 2

Communication Focus 2: Describing Problems and Suggesting Solutions

1. Describe the Problem

Describe or define a problem clearly before attempting to solve it. The following expressions are useful in doing that.

Expressions	Examples
in fact, . . .	My score shows up online as 73; **in fact,** I got 78.
actually, . . .	Yes, Ottawa is the national capital, but **actually,** the capital of Ontario is Toronto.
so . . .	My laptop broke, **so** I cannot finish the essay.
believe it or not, . . .	Dr. Ip's class was cancelled last week. **Believe it or not,** she still expects us to be ready for the test.
unfortunately, . . .	English is a communication tool all around the world. **Unfortunately,** not everyone has the chance to learn it.
have difficulty with (+ noun)	Vlad **has difficulty** with calculus.
have difficulty with (+ gerund)	Giacomo **has difficulty** managing time.
have trouble with (+ noun)	Pilar **is having trouble** with the bus schedule.
have trouble with (+ gerund)	Sami **has trouble** with losing weight.
a problem with (+ noun)	There is **a problem with** text translation.
a problem with (+ gerund)	Tang has **a problem with** waking up in time for class.
an issue of . . .	There is **an issue of** signage with Quebec businesses.
aren't doing/responding to. . .	They **aren't doing** what they said they'd do. They **aren't responding to** our questions.

2. Suggest Solutions

When offering solutions, remember that some ways of expressing this are stronger than others.

Examples:

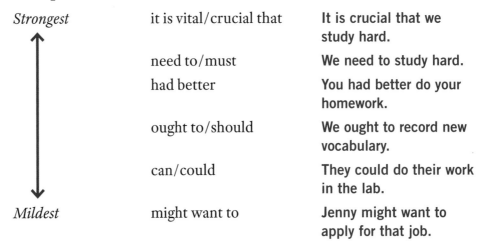

Strongest	it is vital/crucial that	It is crucial that we study hard.
	need to/must	We need to study hard.
	had better	You had better do your homework.
	ought to/should	We ought to record new vocabulary.
	can/could	They could do their work in the lab.
Mildest	might want to	Jenny might want to apply for that job.

SPEAKING ACTIVITY 12

Look around the classroom and choose one object. Describe it to the class with three or four observations. Then, describe what is wrong with it.

Example:

> your chair
>
> **My chair has six parts: the seat, the back, and four legs. The back and seat are made of wood, and the legs are made of metal. It is about a metre and a half tall. I have a problem with this chair. It is too hard, so I get a sore back quickly. Unfortunately, it is not adjustable.**

SPEAKING ACTIVITY 13

In groups, select a problem that you may have observed in, for instance, the school cafeteria, a nearby public building or park, the local bus system, local roads, a local business or service, the local government, etc. When you have agreed on a problem, work together to describe and define it, then brainstorm and discuss solutions.

SPEAKING ACTIVITY 14

Work with your partner to discuss the following situations, using language from Communication Focus 2 to describe the problems and brainstorm solutions.

1. You are a full-time first-year student starting a summer holiday during which you must find a co-op job. You have been offered a hard-to-get job as front desk clerk at the Peach Tree Resort and Spa. The resort wants you to start working full-time on a long-term contract and quit school.

2. You have opened a small business in town. An artistic friend gave you a gift of painting the whole outside wall of your store with beautiful graphics that match the local area and your tastes. Shortly after the painting was completed, you found it covered in graffiti. Your friend generously came back and did some touch-up work to make it look better, but last night someone spray-painted even more graffiti on it.

3. You lent a friend $100. He said he'd pay it back in a week, but actually he paid you back several weeks later, and only after you repeatedly asked him for the money. Today that same friend asks to borrow $75.

4. You left your smartphone on a table in the cafeteria at lunchtime. It has only been an hour, but your phone is gone and the cafeteria is crowded. Moreover, there is a high rate of turnover of people at this time of day. Your phone has not turned up with either the cafeteria staff or the school lost and found.

5. You are the only student from your country in your ESL class. During break time and sometimes even in class your classmates are all speaking their mother tongues with each other.

Speaking STRATEGY

"It is more fun to talk with someone who doesn't use long, difficult words but rather short, easy words like 'What about lunch?'"
—Winnie-the-Pooh

This quote illustrates that the human attention span is short. Keep in mind when you are talking that you don't want to lose your audience's attention. Try to say what you want to say in as few words as possible: be concise.

SPEAKING ACTIVITY 15

Mark the words you know with ✔ and the words you don't know with ✗.
Compare your lists with a partner and help each other understand the
vocabulary by explaining its meaning. Use your dictionary and thesaurus
to help you understand words that neither of you know.

Some Adjectives That Modify the Word *problem*		Some Terms to Use When Describing a Problem	
acute	humanitarian	issue	undermine
grave	big	need	at the root of
serious	enormous	question	at the expense of
deepening	great	crisis	prejudice
growing	huge	controversy	marginalized
impending	minor/major	attribute	
economic	perceived		
financial	complex		
fiscal			

SPEAKING ACTIVITY 16

Make a list of five issues about learning English that you have
encountered. Take turns with your partner to use words from Speaking
Activity 15 to describe the issues in more detail to the class.

Example:

too much new vocabulary

> I have a <u>serious</u> problem. I spend too much time learning new
> vocabulary <u>at the expense of</u> my grammar.

1. _____
2. _____
3. _____
4. _____
5. _____

SPEAKING ACTIVITY 17

Think of a problem that exists in your country or in Canada. Describe
it to your partner. Explain how the problem started and how it affects
people.

Example:

> The inability of sick people to access the medical system is a
> growing issue in my country. This humanitarian crisis started
> when the government started to cut spending on hospitals, and
> now people have to wait six hours for even basic medical care, or
> get none at all.

👥 SPEAKING ACTIVITY 18

With your partner, practise making and then saying sentences that combine words from Speaking Activity 15 with verbs below. Use your dictionary or thesaurus as necessary.

require	overcome	solve	develop
co-operate	build	confront	address

Examples:

> This <u>question requires</u> a lot of thought.
>
> Cesar decided to <u>build</u> an <u>enormous</u> castle out of **LEGO**.

👥👥 SPEAKING ACTIVITY 19

In groups, share the problems you described in Speaking Activities 16 and 17 and discuss solutions that could contribute to ending the problems.

PRONUNCIATION

Pronunciation Focus 1: Recognizing and Using Voiced Sounds

Voiced sounds are made when the vocal cords vibrate. If you hold two fingers to your throat as you talk, you will be able to feel the vibration. All vowels and some consonants are voiced.

👥 PRONUNCIATION ACTIVITY 1

Work with a partner. Practise saying each voiceless sound and then add voice to it and write the sound you hear. Complete the table with the voiced sounds.

For example, the sound / p / is voiceless, but if you make the sound of / p / but add voice, you'll hear / b /. Therefore, / b / is voiced.

Both / p / and / b / are articulated the same way—the only difference is vocal cord vibration.

voiceless	/ p /	/ f /	/ k /	/ s /	/ t /	/ θ /	/ ʃ /	/ tʃ /
voiced								

👥 PRONUNCIATION ACTIVITY 2

Using your answers from Pronunciation Activity 1 as a guide, work with your partner to make lists of word pairs that contrast voiced and voiceless sounds and practise saying them aloud.

Example:

/ p /—/ b /:   pig, big   pack, back   park, bark

Pronunciation Focus 2:
Pronouncing Consonants (-s endings)

 Track 7   One of the most common mistakes of English language learners is not saying the ends of words clearly, particularly final -*s*, which occurs frequently in plurals, the present tense, and possessives.

There are three "rules of thumb" to help speakers decide how to pronounce words accurately.

Rule 1: If the word ends in a voiceless consonant sound: / f /, / k /, / p /, / t /, / θ /, pronounce the *s* as / s /.

> **Examples:** laughs, drinks, mops, doughnuts, myths

Rule 2: If the word ends in a voiced consonant sound: / b /, / d /, / g /, / l /, / m /, / n /, / r /, / ð /, / v /, or a vowel sound, pronounce the *s* as / z /.

> **Examples:** Habs, bids, rags, pills, dreams, cones, hers, bathes, saves, knees

Rule 3: If the word ends with: / s /, / z /, / ʃ /, / tʃ /, / dʒ /, or / ʒ /, pronounce *s* as / ɪz /.

> **Examples:** buses, buzzes, wishes, watches, judges, mirages

👥 PRONUNCIATION ACTIVITY 3

Track 8   Listen and categorize each -*s* ending as a Rule 1, Rule 2, or Rule 3 sound. When you are finished, share your answers with a classmate.

surveys ____	millionaires ____	messages ____	incomes ____
books ____	tablets ____	quarters ____	months ____
retailers ____	laptops ____	wages ____	places ____
values ____	grounds ____	doubts ____	questions ____
dollars ____	choices ____	differences ____	colleges ____

👥 PRONUNCIATION ACTIVITY 4

With a partner, add four common nouns to each final -*s* type. Use the chart on the next page. When you are finished, share your answers with your class and add your classmates' words to your list.

-/ s /	-/ z /	-/ ɪz /
cats	dogs	foxes

PRONUNCIATION ACTIVITY 5

A. Listen to the news story about millionaires shopping. As you listen, circle word endings in the news story that have the final *-s* sounds:

/ s /, / z /, and / ɪz /.

Note! Focus on sounds, not spelling: sometimes even a word that ends in *e*, like ***finance***, has a final / s / sound.

 **Track 9**

B. Now, read the news story out loud to your partner and identify the final *-s* sounds as one of these:

Rule 1: / s /

Rule 2: / z / or

Rule 3: / ɪz /

by writing the correct numbers above the circles you made.

Canadian Millionaires Shop at Walmart

Forget about one's affluence, it's the price that counts—according to a 2016 survey that shows millionaires are just like us: they love shopping at Walmart.

Like us, millionaires spend their dollars on clothes, food products, cosmetics, drinks, cars, car maintenance, computers, laptops, and tablets. Two-thirds of the millionaires interviewed shopped more often at Walmart stores than at The Bay or Sears.

For many reasons, we respect millionaires and hunt for tips and ideas on the spending habits that make them rich, and it's fun to consider the similarities and differences between millionaires and the rest of us in terms of salaries and shopping choices. Nevertheless, one thing is certain: it's obvious that all of us try to get the best value for our dollars and cents.

Pronunciation Focus 3: Pronouncing Consonants (-*ed* endings)

 **Track 10**

As with -*s* endings, -*ed* endings are common and often not pronounced clearly by English language learners. The three rules for pronouncing -*ed* are similar to those of -*s*.

Rule 1: If the word ends in a voiceless consonant sound: / s /, / f /, / k /, / p /, / ʃ /, / θ /, / tʃ /, pronounce -*ed* as / t /.

> **Examples:** missed, laughed, liked, slipped, wished, unearthed, watched

Rule 2: If the word ends in a voiced consonant sound: / b /, / g /, / l /, / m /, / n /, / r /, / ð /, / v /, / z /, / dʒ /, / ʒ /, or a vowel sound, pronounce -*ed* as / d /.

> **Examples:** robbed, hugged, called, combed, scanned, stirred, bathed, loved, prioritized, judged, avenged, cried, stayed, allowed

Rule 3: If the word already ends with / d / or / t /: pronounce -*ed* as / ɪd /.

> **Examples:** needed, heated, embedded, regulated, legislated, conceded

👥 PRONUNCIATION ACTIVITY 6

 Track 11

Listen and categorize each -*ed* ending as a Rule 1, Rule 2, or Rule 3 sound. Practise saying the words as you complete the exercise. Share your answers with your partner.

worked ____	played ____	wanted ____	jumped ____
needed ____	lived ____	studied ____	risked ____
watched ____	loved ____	kissed ____	tasted ____
believed ____	feared ____	invited ____	

👤 PRONUNCIATION ACTIVITY 7

Track 12

Listen to and repeat each sentence, focusing on accurate word endings. Circle the word that you hear.

1. Can you lend me your (cart/card)?
2. Place the (bet/bed) over here.
3. I (work/worked) a lot with my sister.
4. We (live/lived) in Saskatoon.
5. The files we needed were (scant/scanned).
6. Have you (built/billed) the company?

👤 PRONUNCIATION ACTIVITY 8A

Track 13

Listen to and repeat each word or phrase, taking care to enunciate properly.

stayed home	texted you	ordered pizza
watched TV	missed you	finished my homework
surfed the net	wanted to	walked over
danced all night	busted	

PRONUNCIATION ACTIVITY 8B

Listen to the following conversations, then act out one of the dialogues with your partner in front of the class.

 **Track 14**

Dialogue 1

Fred: Hi, Wendy, it's Fred.

Wendy: Oh, hi, Fred.

Fred: Hey Wendy, what did you do yesterday? Did you go out? I texted you . . .

Wendy: I stayed home. I ordered pizza and watched TV.

Fred: Darn, I'm sorry I missed you. I should've walked over.

Wendy: I guess.

Fred: So you stayed home? Me too.

Wendy: What did you do?

Fred: I finished my homework and surfed the net a little.

Wendy: Sweet. Too bad I didn't check my messages. I wanted to hang out with you.

Fred: Oh? But I checked on Facebook! You danced all night with Arshad!

Wendy: Oops! Busted!

Dialogue 2

Julie: Hi, Steve. How was your holiday?

Steve: Great. I travelled to Bermuda.

Julie: That sounds like fun. I stayed here and studied and worked.

Steve: That's too bad. But Bermuda was great. I got up early and watched the sun rise every morning.

Julie: Nice. I never stopped. Work was so busy.

Steve: I know, I was thinking about you as I walked along Elbow Beach.

Julie: Well I hope you remembered to put on sunscreen.

Steve: Yeah, but I messed up. I forgot about my feet and burned them.

Julie: Ouch, yeah, I see you're wearing sandals.

Dialogue 3

Taylor: Good morning, how are you?

Ryan: I'm well, thank you. I didn't think you remembered me. We met last night at the cocktail party.

Taylor: I'm terribly sorry, I remembered your face, but not your name.

Ryan: We talked about my invention, the duck boat.

Taylor: Yes, we discussed strategies for marketing pitches.

Ryan: You liked it and commented that you wanted to see a prototype.

Taylor: I mentioned it to my manager and she wasn't interested.

Ryan: That's okay, I'm sorry I wasted your time.

Taylor: No need to apologize, I enjoyed speaking with you.

Pronunciation Focus 4: Pronouncing Vowel Sounds

 **Track 15**

All vowel sounds are voiced. They are classified by their area of articulation in the mouth, which is either front, central, or back.

	FRONT	CENTRAL	BACK
High	i		u
	ɪ		ʊ
Mid	eɪ	ə ɚ	oʊ ɔɪ
	ɛ	ʌ	
Low	æ	aɪ aʊ	ɑ

1. Front Vowels

Look at these front vowel sounds and their example words. Note the area of articulation of these front vowel sounds in the diagram as you listen to the audio:

/ i /	as in m<u>ee</u>t
/ ɪ /	as in m<u>i</u>tt
/ eɪ /	as in m<u>a</u>te
/ ɛ /	as in m<u>e</u>t
/ æ /	as in m<u>a</u>t

 PRONUNCIATION ACTIVITY 9

 **Track 16**

A. Listen to and repeat each word out loud.

/ i /	/ ɪ /	/ eɪ /	/ ɛ /	/ æ /
seat	sit	sate	set	sat
been	bin	bane	Ben	ban
meek	Mick	make	men	mac
heal	hill	hail	hell	Hal

B. With a partner, add as many words as you can think of that use the same front vowel sounds.

 **PRONUNCIATION ACTIVITY 10**

 **Track 17**

A. Read the dialogue on the next page and underline all front vowels (the first two lines have already been done).

B. Write all the front vowel words from the dialogue in the appropriate boxes in the chart. Compare your answers with those of your partner.

C. Listen to the dialogue and practise it out loud with your partner.

Dialogue

Anna: Hey Steve, ready?

Steve: Uh huh. Hi, Anna. I've been ready since last term. I'm studying math for the last time.

Anna: You and Ben, he's registered too.

Steve: Oh yeah, I see him sitting over there. He has his headphones on.

Anna: Yeah. Looks like he's singing.

Steve: And the teacher's going over to his seat! She's asking Ben to leave!!

Anna: Hmm. Maybe Ben isn't registered.

Steve: No, Anna, I just think he's a really bad singer.

Sound	/i/	/ɪ/	/eɪ/	/ɛ/	/æ/
Words from dialogue	Steve been ready studying	since	hey	ready	Anna last math

👥 **PRONUNCIATION ACTIVITY 11**

Work with a partner and use your list of vocabulary from Pronunciation Activity 10 to create your own dialogue.

Example:

/i/ been, he, teacher   /ɪ/ since, sit, his, sing

/eɪ/ hey   /ɛ/ Ben, register, headphones

/æ/ ask, math, Anna

Person A: Did you know that Ben and Anna have been teaching math since last year?

Person B: I had no idea. I thought they were teaching English.

Person A: . . .

2. Central Vowels

Look at these central vowel sounds and their example words. Note the area of articulation of these central vowel sounds in the diagram at the top of page 26 as you listen to the audio:

 Track 18

/ə/   as in Canada   /ʌ/   as in truck   /aʊ/   as in house

/ɚ/   as in girl   /aɪ/   as in bike

🎧 PRONUNCIATION ACTIVITY 12

Fill in the chart with at least two more words in each column that use central vowel sounds. When you are finished, compare your words with a partner.

/ ə /	/ ɚ /	/ ʌ /	/ aɪ /	/ aʊ /
about	lurk	luck	like	mouse
idea	hurt	hut	lot	found

3. Back Vowels

🎧 Track 19

Look at these back vowel sounds and their example words. Note the area of articulation of these back vowel sounds in the diagram below as you listen to the audio:

/ u /	as in rule	/ ɔɪ /	as in boy	/ oʊ /	as in own
/ ʊ /	as in took	/ ɑ /	as in saw		

	FRONT	CENTRAL	BACK
High	i		u
	ɪ		ʊ
Mid	eɪ	ə ɚ	oʊ ɔɪ
	ɛ	ʌ	
Low	æ	aɪ aʊ	ɑ

🎧 PRONUNCIATION ACTIVITY 13

Work with a partner to fill in the chart with at least two more words for each of the same vowel sounds.

/ u /	/ ʊ /	/ oʊ /	/ ɔɪ /	/ ɑ /
fool	full	foal	foil	fall
sued	should	sowed	soy	sawed

COMMUNICATING IN THE REAL WORLD

Here is an opportunity to use English to talk to people outside your class. Work in a small group to make up a questionnaire asking five or six questions about **one** of the interesting topics below.

To improve your questionnaire, practise asking your questions to other groups to make sure they can understand the meaning of what you are asking. Show your revised questions to your teacher. Before you start the actual survey, practise your delivery in small groups of classmates. After you have completed the actual survey, report back to the class what you found.

Topics:

English as a global language

Protecting the English language

What's wrong with the English language?

The benefits of language learning

The struggles of language learners

SELF-EVALUATION

Think about your work in this chapter. For each row in the chart sections **Grammar and Language Functions**, **Pronunciation**, **Learning Strategies**, and **Note-Taking**, give yourself a score based on the rating scale below and write a comment in the Notes section.

Show the chart to your teacher. Talk about what you need to do to make your English better.

Rating Scale

| 1 | 2 | 3 | 4 | 5 |

Needs improvement. ←——————————————→ *Great!*

	Score	Notes
Grammar and Language Functions		
describing by classifying		
describing with participial adjectives		
matching verb tenses with the time of the context		
describing problems and suggesting solutions		

Pronunciation

recognizing and using voiced sounds		
pronouncing consonants (-*s* endings)		
pronouncing consonants (-*ed* endings)		
pronouncing vowel sounds		

Learning Strategies

Speaking

being concise to keep the listener's attention		

Listening

identifying a speaker's intent		
previewing questions before listening to build context		
focusing on ideas rather than words		

Note-Taking

using a chart to connect notes to speakers		
identifying varying points of view		

Vocabulary and Language Chunks

Look at this list of new vocabulary and language chunks you learned in this chapter. Give yourself a score based on the rating scale and write a comment.

Globish	democratize	legislate	cultural roots
mother tongue	concession	descriptive	draw a distinction
Hinglish	deplore	prescriptive	default to something
colonist	diversity	ascertain	the nature of
imperialism	infiltrate	etymology	pecking order
dominant	dominant	futile	make an impression on
lingua franca	embedded	self-regulating	the final word
multilingual	regulate	replicate	the tip of the iceberg
linguistic		derivatives	
denounce			
nuance			

	Score	Notes
understanding new vocabulary and language chunks		
using new lexical items freely and confidently		

My plan for practising is _____

_____

_____

CHAPTER 2

Communication Technology

Asking questions to gather information

Summarizing information

Paraphrasing information

Expressing an analysis

THINKING AND TALKING

Working in small groups, look at the pictures and discuss the following questions. What is happening in each picture? Do you think there are any issues with language here? Explain. What differences are there between Internet language and everyday spoken language? Is there a degeneration of language because of the Internet? Can texting and tweeting be good for language? Explain.

LISTENING 1

Before You Listen

👥 PRE-LISTENING ACTIVITY

What do you think the proverb "The more things change, the more things stay the same" means? Use your answers from the previous task to discuss with a partner how you think the English language has changed because of the Internet.

UPFRONT VOCABULARY

precedent	an action or decision that happened in the past and is seen as an example or rule to be followed in a similar situation*
degeneration	the process of becoming worse or less acceptable in quality or condition*
dialect	the form of a language that is spoken in one geographical area with aspects such as grammar, words, and pronunciation that may be different from other forms of the same language spoken in other areas*
perception	the idea, belief, or message that one has as a result of how one sees something*

forum   a place where people can exchange opinions and
                    ideas on a particular issue*

spectrum   a complete, wide range of related qualities, ideas, etc.*

counterintuitive   the opposite of what you would expect or what seems
                    to be obvious*

*Definition courtesy of *Oxford Advanced Learner's Dictionary*.

👥 PRE-LISTENING VOCABULARY

A. Use a dictionary and work with a partner to decide which word or
   words in each row are not synonyms of the target vocabulary in
   bold, then cross out the words that do not belong.

Listening STRATEGY 🔊

Make a **pre-listening plan**. Use the information you have (the title, a picture, your knowledge of the topic, and what you think the audience's needs are) to anticipate what the speaker is going to say and what kind of organization the speaker will likely use.

   Example:

   renowned   well-known   ~~purchased~~   famous   prominent

   brainwashed programmed   influenced   conditioned   cleaned
   devastating impactful   destructive   destroying   hypocritical
   expressive quick   animated   meaningful   showy
   intriguing relaxing   interesting   fascinating   stimulating
   essentially normally   basically   really   fundamentally
   deteriorate degenerate   worsen   weaken   insult
   alter   change   design   vary   revise
   constrain   limit   move   restrict   confine
   prompt (v.) trigger   encourage   provoke   accept

B. Practise using the target vocabulary by creating complete sentences
   with each of them. Share your sentences with your class.

Note-Taking

When taking notes, you can save space and time in the following ways.

A. Use symbols and abbreviations.

   Complete the chart and add your own favourites in the blank spaces,
   then compare your list with that of a partner. Add anything to your
   chart from your classmates' lists that you find helpful.

&	and	#		↓		∴			
=	equal to	/		→					
@		*		<					
?		↑		>					
w.		e.g.		i.e.		p.		K	
w/o		b/c		p/u		s/o		C	

B. Use the first few letters of the word (and/or remove the vowels).

Guess the meaning of the following abbreviations and short forms. When you are finished, compare your answers with those of your partner.

max.	min.	re.	mgmt	info.	lang.
pol.	abbr.	etc.	incl.	econ.	edu.
gov.	dept.	pres.	cont.	sth	mkt
Cdn	esp.	approx.	sb		

 Track 20 In the interview "Internet Linguistics: How We Use Language Online," David Crystal, world-renowned linguist and author of "Texting" and *Language and the Internet*, looks at the effect of the Internet on language. What do you predict he will say about language change?

As you listen to "Internet Linguistics: How We Use Language Online" for the first time, practise taking notes using as many short forms as you can.

Listening for the Main Ideas

 Track 21 Listen to the interview "Internet Linguistics" once again and add to your notes. Then use your notes to answer the questions. When you are finished, compare your answers with those of a classmate.

1. What does Mr. Crystal say to people who worry that texting and tweeting cause degeneration of language?
2. Explain how Internet linguistics is "counterintuitive."
3. How does Mr. Crystal predict that the Internet will change?
4. Give an example of how technology constrains language.

Listening Comprehension

 **Track 22** **A.** Read the seven questions, and then listen again to the interview "Internet Linguistics," pausing as necessary but without rewinding. Write the answers for the questions as you hear them.

B. When you are finished, compare your answers with those of a classmate.

1. Q: How do people react to changes in language?

   A: Whenever new technology comes along, people _____

   _____.

2. Q: What is Internet linguistics more like, speaking or writing?

   A: It is _____.

3. Q: What is probably going to happen to the Internet over the next 10 years, according to David Crystal?

   A: It's going to become _____.

4. Q: Which style of English has the Internet extended the most, formal or informal language?

   A: It has extended _____.

5. Q: What have most ordinary people realized after about 10 years of Internet linguistics?

   A: They've realized that 99.9 percent _____

   _____.

6. Q: What did Twitter change in 2009 that made it much more of a news reporting medium?

   A: Twitter changed _____.

7. Q: What is the example Crystal gives of people's playfulness with language on the Internet?

   A: People _____.

Personalizing

Work with your group to create a lexicon (vocabulary list) of all the English "text speak" that you and your group mates know. As you compile your list, share your thoughts with your group about the items you are recording. For each, consider its appropriateness, effectiveness, longevity (how long it will be used) and impact. Finally, post your list on the board or online for comparison with other groups' work.

Term	Meaning	Appropriateness casual, friendly, formal	Effectiveness high, medium, low	Longevity high, medium, low	Impact high, medium, low
LOL	laugh out loud	casual/friendly	medium	high	high

Vocabulary and Language Chunks

Complete the sentences from the interview using the language chunks in the left-hand column. Use your understanding of grammatical patterns to help you with your choices. When you've finished, compare your answers with those of a partner and work together to build other sentences using the same expressions.

Language Chunks	Examples
1. a good example is . . .	You know, it's part of _____ the medium.
2. to a considerable extent	The language has become increasingly conversational _____.
3. has a (playful) dimension	It's difficult to _____ the Internet as a whole.
4. is predominantly (written)	That was really _____ the book I originally wrote 10 years ago.
5. the novelty of . . .	_____ just because a usage is now, it will be the same in a year's time.
6. an expanding array of . . .	But all language _____, of course.
7. the motivation behind . . .	But on the Internet, which _____, you can see it all over the place.
8. you can't assume that . . .	And __1__ the way people are prepared to create new words.
9. make generalizations about . . .	It is all part of _____ linguistic possibilities.

Write your sentences here:

_____

_____

_____

_____

_____

_____

_____

_____

_____

_____

SPEAKING 1

Communication Focus 1:
Asking Questions to Gather Information

Asking questions is part of the investigatory process. In this chapter, you will learn to ask questions thoughtfully and confidently.

1. Closed Questions

This type of question limits the number of potential responses, for example, yes/no, multiple choice, or short-answer questions.

Examples:

> Did you get the notes from the last lecture?
>
> What is the capital of Prince Edward Island?
>
> Where do you come from?

2. Open Questions

This question type does not limit the potential responses and provides a context for the respondent to answer with his or her own opinions.

Examples:

> How do you feel about posting your personal pictures on Facebook?
>
> Why do you think it is important to use good grammar in public?
>
> How would you describe your experience in Canada so far?

3. Indirect Questions

In academic and formal contexts, **indirect questions** are an alternative way to ask a question. Notice how the word order is different in the sentence pairs below.

Examples:

> When does the lecture start? (direct)
>
> Do you know when the lecture starts? (indirect)

> How did you set up your Instagram account? (direct)
>
> Could you tell me how you set up your Instagram account? (indirect)

> When did people start using "there is . . ." as a plural? (direct)
>
> I would like to know when people started using "there is" as a plural. (indirect)

> Why don't you use Facebook? (direct)
>
> May I ask you why you don't use Facebook? (indirect)

> Is the Internet changing language for the worse? (direct)
>
> I wonder if the Internet is changing language for the worse. (indirect)

ŇŇŇ SPEAKING ACTIVITY 1

Play a quiz game with your group mates. Each group member writes a closed, direct question on a card until each group has a total of 10 question cards. Have the teacher check your cards for accuracy, then exchange question cards with another group, keeping the cards face down. Now, in each group, one student will randomly choose a card, select a "questioner" within the group, and whisper the question to that person. That questioner must then invert the question, changing it to an indirect question, and ask the question of the rest of the group.

Example:

Person A (to Person B): **When did Newfoundland become the 10th province?**

Person B (to group): <u>**Could you tell me when Newfoundland became the 10th province.**</u>

Grammar Note: Using Interrogatives

Remember that most yes/no questions are formed by inverting the subject and the auxiliary (helping) verb.

Examples:

She's on Facebook.   ➔   Is she on Facebook?

You are busy.   ➔   Are you busy? (Am I busy?)

We will finish soon.   ➔   Will we finish soon?

Carlos is studying.   ➔   Is Carlos studying?

The Canadiens are winning!   ➔   Are the Canadiens winning?

They've finished.   ➔   Have they finished?

The parcel has arrived.   ➔   Has the parcel arrived?

We can go now.   ➔   Can we go now?

If there is no helping verb (that is, if the verb is in the simple past or present), invert using ***do***, ***does***, or ***did***.

Examples:

They study French.   ➔   Do they study French?

The lecture starts at five.   ➔   Does the lecture start at five?

We visited Truro.   ➔   Did you visit Truro?

To make ***wh-*** questions, put ***who***, ***what***, ***when***, ***where***, or ***how*** before the inversion.

Examples:

Do they study . . .   ➔   What do they study?

Does the lecture start at . . .   ➔   When does the lecture start?

Did you visit . . .   ➔   Where did you visit?

Questions about the sentence below are inverted with the helping verb *did*. Note that the subject question (1) is not inverted.

Example:

<u>Harry</u> <u>baked</u> <u>a cake</u> <u>in the kitchen</u> <u>for Sammy</u> <u>yesterday</u> <u>because he likes baking</u>.
  1   2   3   4   5   6   7

1. Who baked a cake?
2. What did Harry do?
3. What did Harry bake?
4. Where did Harry bake the cake?
5. Who did Harry bake the cake for?
6. When did Harry bake the cake?
7. Why did Harry bake the cake?

👥 SPEAKING ACTIVITY 2

Work in small groups for this game. One person in the group is the riddler. The riddler imagines a famous person, place, or thing. The other group members take turns to ask him or her up to 20 questions that can be answered with either *yes* or *no*.

When one group member guesses the answer to the riddle, it is that person's turn to be the riddler and choose a famous person, place, or thing. If no one guesses correctly after 20 questions, the riddler gets to be the riddler again and choose another famous person, place, or thing.

Strategies:

- A good strategy for organizing your questions is to shift from general to specific. For instance, ask, "Is the person from Europe?" before asking "Is he or she from France?"
- Build on your successes: if the answer to a question that the previous group mate asked was yes, ask more specific questions along the same line; however, if the answer was no, change the direction of your questioning.

👥 SPEAKING ACTIVITY 3

A decision tree helps illustrate a step-by-step question-based approach to decision-making. For questions that can be answered with a yes/no answer, the thought process can be illustrated with a decision tree similar to the one in the photo, where you can see the question to be answered is: "Are you happy?" From there, you have two possible answer choices that lead to the next yes/no question, and so on until there is a resolution to the initial question.

With **wh-** questions that are more open, the decision tree can be more complex, and the creator of the diagram can be more creative.

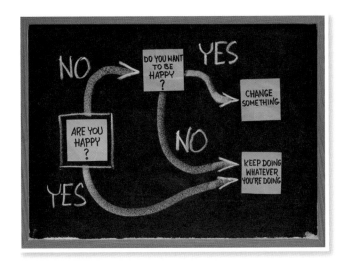

Work together with a partner and create your own decision tree diagram for one of the following topics. Your decision tree should have at least two steps (see picture). When you are finished, share it with your class.

Extension activity: Search online for a decision tree and share it with your class the next day.

Topics for your decision tree:

1. Should I post this picture on Facebook?
2. Should I check my email?
3. What music should I listen to right now?
4. Where should I go on holiday?
5. What should I study?
6. Choose your own: _____

👥 SPEAKING ACTIVITY 4

Work together with a partner to change the following closed questions into more open discussion questions. When you are finished, practise asking and then discussing your open questions with your partner.

Example:

Closed: **Do you think it is important to use good grammar in conversation?**

Open: **Why do you think using good grammar is important in conversation?**

1. Did you get the notes from the last lecture?
2. Have I answered your question?
3. Is it okay with you if we study at the student pub?
4. Are you comfortable with this option?
5. Did you post that picture on Facebook?

👥 SPEAKING ACTIVITY 5

Ask your partner about his or her Internet activities and preferences, for example, web surfing, social media, or favourite apps. Use indirect questions like those you've already learned in this chapter to add a more formal tone.

👥 SPEAKING ACTIVITY 6

Divide the class into four teams of at least four people per team. Your teacher will give each team a picture from a four-part story to look at. The teams will then compete to see which one will be the first to piece together the whole story. To begin, each team assigns one or two team members to be a "host" (or hosts) to stay with its picture (kept hidden) to answer questions; the rest of the team acts as the "investigators." The investigators go to each of the other groups' hosts asking questions (direct and indirect) about their hidden pictures. (Note: the hosts must never actually show their team's picture to investigators from other teams.) After all investigators have finished asking questions, they return to their team's table and share their findings with the other team members, so that the team can try to piece the whole story together. The goal is to be the first team to determine the sequence of the four-part story, describing which part it has and identifying which parts are with the other teams.

 SPEAKING ACTIVITY 7

In groups of three or four, brainstorm a topic related to this chapter's theme of communications technology and prepare five questions of various types (open/closed, direct/indirect) on it. When your questions are ready, follow the same procedure as in Speaking Activity 6, sending "investigators" to other groups to ask them your questions. After your investigators have met with every group, they should return and report the answers they have gathered to their own groups. Finally, each group will summarize its findings for the class.

Communication Focus 2: Summarizing Information

We summarize in order to highlight the main ideas of what we heard or saw, so summaries are often in the past tense. Speakers do this regularly in daily interactions as well as in formal situations at the end of presentations.

Some of the structures that are often used for summarizing are:

> **In summary,** Franklin's theory supported the new initiatives.
>
> **The main points were that** cars polluted the air and created significant landfill.
>
> **The most important issues were that** technology is changing rapidly and people can't keep up.
>
> **To conclude, the information presented** deepened my understanding of the topic.
>
> **In a nutshell,** Einstein's theories are quite complicated.
>
> **To sum it all up,** cell phone usage has become quite a significant social issue.
>
> **The speaker said/meant/implied** that languages change mostly for the better.

 SPEAKING ACTIVITY 8

Join each of the following beginning phrases with an ending from the list below. Then put the completed sentences into an order that makes sense to you. When you are finished, compare your summary with another pair.

1. In a nutshell, I learned that
2. I'm quite certain the speaker implied that

3. On the other hand, I learned that
4. If people communicate in this way,
5. The most important issue regarding language change is that

_____ communication styles will become more efficient.

_____ the use of social networking can make language ambiguous.

_____ there were clearly two sides to this argument.

_____ more and more people communicate using fewer characters.

_____ communicating using fewer characters isn't necessarily a bad thing.

SPEAKING ACTIVITY 9

A. Ask your classmates about their preferences. Decide on an area of interest, for example, social media, foods, pastimes, mobile devices, TV shows, music or movie genres, etc., and prepare a survey question.

Ask your question to as many classmates as time allows and tally your findings.

Example: What social media do you prefer?

B. Use the data to summarize your findings using the summarizing language from Communication Focus 2 above. Draw some informal conclusions about your classmates' choices and present your summary to the class.

Communication Focus 3: Paraphrasing Information

We paraphrase in order to express a speaker's or writer's idea in our own, different words. A good paraphrase keeps the original idea, but makes it easier to understand.

These are the three principles of effective paraphrasing:

1. Trust your notes and memory to compose your paraphrase.
2. Begin your paraphrase with the subject or topic.
3. Ensure the original message does not get distorted.

Grammar Note: Using Reported Speech

Reported speech is a common grammatical pattern used in paraphrasing. Reported speech involves

- changing the verb tense and
- changing the person of the pronoun.

Common reporting verbs include _say, tell, state, answer, respond, reply,_ and _argue._ You may add the word _that_ after the reporting verb.

CHANGE TENSES

1. **Present to past:**

   Sam said, "I want to study in Sue's class." → Sam said <u>he</u> <u>wanted</u> to study in Sue's class.

   Olivia stated, "I'm working hard." → Olivia stated <u>she</u> <u>was</u> <u>work</u>ing hard.

   Note: If what was stated is still true, it is acceptable to leave it in the present tense.

   Junko answered, "It is Monday." → Junko answered it was Monday.

   or

   → Junko answered it is Monday. (if still true)

2. **Past to past perfect:**

   Angel argued, "Sarah won the case." → Angel argued Sarah had won the case.

   Enrique said, "Hassam saw the report." → Enrique said Hassam had seen the report.

   Note: In conversational English, this rule is often ignored and simple past is used.

   Enrique said, "Hassam saw the report." → Enrique said Hassam saw the report.

CHANGE PRONOUNS

Examples:

She said, "<u>I</u> want <u>this</u>." → She said <u>she</u> wanted <u>that</u>.

Honoré reported, "<u>We</u> have finished." → Honoré reported <u>they</u> had finished.

ADD *THAT*

Examples:

She said, "My friend worked all day." → She said <u>that</u> her friend had worked all day.

Antoine replied, "It's too expensive." → Antoine replied <u>that</u> it was too expensive.

👥 **SPEAKING ACTIVITY 10**

With your partner, paraphrase the following statements using reported speech. When you are finished, check your answers with the class.

1. Nadja murmured: "I am intrigued."

   _____

2. Daniel whispered: "I studied a lot last night."

   _____

3. Guillermo stated: "I am going to be absent."

_____

4. Stephanie responded: "I do my homework every day."

_____

5. Shin Seung specified: "I live in Seoul, South Korea."

_____

👥 SPEAKING ACTIVITY 11

With your partner, choose one of the paragraphs below and work together to paraphrase it, applying the three principles of effective paraphrasing (trust your notes and memory; begin with the subject or topic; make sure that the original message is not altered):

Paragraph 1

According to David Crystal, ". . . in other words, you know, new ways of talking and communicating come along. The Internet has given us, oh, 10 or 15 new styles of communication: long messages like blogging, and then short messages like texting and tweeting. So I see it as all as part of an expanding array of linguistic possibilities."

Paragraph 2

According to Nora Young, ". . . you have 140 characters on Twitter so that's going to affect the way you present yourself. But is that unique to the Internet? Or has whatever the dominant technology always affected the way we communicate, whether it's you know, slate or stone tablets or whatever?"

👥 SPEAKING ACTIVITY 12

Work with your partner to practise rephrasing the following sentences, prefacing them with one of the expressions from the speaking strategy. Use your dictionary as necessary to find synonyms. Express your answers to your class or teacher.

Example:

Cash assets are not cultivated within arboreal settings.

Rephrase: **I mean to say that, money doesn't grow on trees.**

1. Broadcasting comes along in the 1920s and people panic because they think everybody's going to be brainwashed.
2. The big thing that's going to happen over the next 10 years is that the Internet's going to become increasingly audio.
3. I mean on the World Wide Web, for instance, there's an awful lot of formal communication.
4. Twitter and smartphones have become mainstream.
5. As soon as a new medium comes along, people start using it and there is this moral panic that associates with it.

Speaking STRATEGY 💬

Sometimes, when it appears that the listener has not understood what you've said, it is helpful to rephrase a sentence. You can restate using different words (synonyms) and begin your rephrase with expressions such as:

In other words . . .

I mean . . .

What I meant to say is . . .

LISTENING 2

Before You Listen

👥 PRE-LISTENING ACTIVITY 1

Discuss the following points with a classmate.

1. Define *social media* and make a list of different types that you use on a daily basis.

2. How have social media helped or hindered you in adjusting to life away from home?

3. Do you think social media make us, as humans, closer to each other or more distant?

👥 PRE-LISTENING ACTIVITY 2

What do you think is a more meaningful discussion, virtual dialogue via social media, or face-to-face dialogue?

Discuss within small groups using phrases like these:

> I believe that . . .
>
> In my experience . . .
>
> As far as I'm concerned . . .
>
> It has been suggested that . . .

UPFRONT VOCABULARY

CD	abbreviation for *compact disc*, a disc on which sound or information is recorded*
Caracas	the capital city of Venezuela
concentrated [juice]	made stronger because water or other substances have been removed*

*Definition courtesy of *Oxford Advanced Learner's Dictionary*.

👥 PRE-LISTENING VOCABULARY

 Track 23

A. Listen to these five excerpts or parts from the narrative that you will hear on the audio and complete the sentences with the words that you hear.

1. Social media means we now have a _____ people we might otherwise avoid.

2. It [social media] transcends the _____ geography.

3. At home we spoke _____ in Spanish and my mom cooked traditional meals.

4. As a kid there wasn't much I could do _____ these conflicting emotions.

5. _____ that doing so brings me double the joy, double the sadness. . .

B. Collocations are word pairings that are used frequently. We often expect these words to be paired together in spoken or written language. This kind of relationship can be seen in several kinds of word pairings, such as noun/verb pairings and adjective/noun pairings:

do <u>homework</u> and *give* <u>advice</u> (verb/noun collocations)

<u>sunny</u> *day* and <u>burnt</u> *toast* (adjective/noun collocations)

Work with a classmate and match the likely collocations below.

Hint: The words from the previous activity are among the collocations.

1. proximity to
2. resolve
3. exclusive
4. constraints of
5. acknowledge

a. fully ~; ~ that; refuse to ~; fail to ~
b. ~ an airport; ~ a school; ~ people; ~ Toronto
c. ~ time; ~ space; ~ geography
d. attempt to ~; try to ~; fail to ~; ~ a problem
e. socially ~; become ~; remain ~; mutually ~

Listening STRATEGY

When possible, synthesize the information you have gained from the listening with what you know about the topic and speaker to make a personal connection. This will trigger ideas and thought processes that will help you remember details more easily, and it will lead you to discover new perspectives and insights into the topic.

Note-Taking

Track 24

Communication technology is such a huge part of everyday life that sometimes it can affect your physical reality. You will listen to a narrative called "Living in Two Worlds." It is a personal story of a young woman who emigrated from one country to live and work in another. Caro Rolando found herself spending more time online with friends and family from her native country than with the real people surrounding her in her everyday life in her new home country of Canada.

When someone is narrating, they often introduce themselves, provide some background, then explain what the problem is or was, give a possible solution to the problem, and conclude with a final thought for the listener to consider. Listen to the complete narrative for the first time and, thinking about the chronological organization of a narrative, take notes in point form using the chart on the next page.

Background:
Problem:
Solution:
Final thoughts:

Listening for the Main Ideas

While listening again to the narrative "Living in Two Worlds," add further information to the notes you have already started, then use your notes to answer the main idea questions.

 **Track 25**

1. Where is the speaker, Caro, from?
2. What was the problem Caro faced?
3. What was the solution she discovered in the early 2000s?
4. How does Caro feel about Dr. Susan Muller's solution?

Listening Comprehension

Listen to the audio again, pausing as necessary (but not rewinding), and answer the questions. When you are finished, compare your answers with a partner and discuss any differences you may have.

 **Track 26**

1. What year did Caro move to Canada?
2. Where in Canada did she move to?
3. How old was she when she moved to Canada?
4. How did Caro and her mom feel about the process of relocating?
5. What did "becoming Canadian" mean for Caro?
6. How did communication technology become a big part of Caro's life? Give examples.
7. Why were social media becoming problematic for Caro after 2010?
8. What is Caro's suggestion for living in two worlds?

Personalizing

Review your notes, thinking about what you have learned. Work with a classmate to create two or three questions based on your own experiences communicating with friends and family at a distance. Share your questions with the other pairs and try to answer each other's questions to the best of your ability.

Vocabulary and Language Chunks

A. Using a dictionary, write definitions of the following vocabulary from Listening 2. Then share your definitions with a classmate.

Example:

disengaging (adj.)   freeing sb/sth from the person/thing that is holding them/it

1. graduate school
2. relocation
3. Skype/Twitter
4. perplex
5. transcend
6. authentic

B. Use a dictionary to learn the meaning of the following language chunks from Listening 2, then create your own sentences with them and share them with a classmate. Practise speaking your sentences aloud.

Example:

concentrated juice: I prefer fresh to concentrated mango juice.

1. to have a point
2. to engage with
3. to immerse oneself in
4. to log on
5. to make do
6. to strike up a conversation

SPEAKING 2

Communication Focus 4: Expressing an Analysis

The language of analysis involves phrases that speakers use to

- state facts
- make informed opinions

Facts: State Similarities, Contrasts, Relationships, and Patterns

Use words that show meaningful relationships:

> Our virtual and physical <u>relationships</u> can be viewed as an equally fabulous reality.

> Social media <u>means</u> we now have a proximity to people.

> Venezuela, <u>where</u> home <u>meant</u> falling asleep to the humming of traffic . . .

> <u>Just as</u> my friends in Toronto would be impressed, my family would be disappointed.

Stress key discourse markers (*but*, *now*, *and*, etc.) that indicate similarity, contrast, or relationships:

> <u>But</u>, at the age of four my mom and I moved to Canada.

> <u>Now</u>, we are armed with a solid defence.

> <u>And</u>, broadcasting comes along in the 1920s and people panic . . .

Informed Opinions: Make Judgments

The language you used to express your opinion will vary, based on the comprehensiveness of the data you have analyzed. Below are some examples of expressions you can use to begin your statements of opinion.

Confident Expression (based on comprehensive data)	Less Confident Expression (relying on insufficient data)
It is clear that . . .	According to my understanding . . .
Obviously/Clearly, . . .	What I discovered is that . . .
There is no doubt that . . .	My analysis is that . . .
Without a doubt . . . The facts show/indicate . . .	Therefore, I believe that . . . So, I think we can determine that . . .

👥 SPEAKING ACTIVITY 13

1. Read the article on the next page, "How Anonymous Are You Online?"

2. Work with your partner to circle key words that identify the main ideas of this passage.

3. Discuss with your partner what you know about this topic (local politics, privacy rights, online posting). How does what you know help you understand it? Has the speaker (the writer) stated ideas that conflict with what you know about this topic?

4. Considering what the writer's message is, what you know, and the facts of the text, work with your partner to make informed opinions about the passage using terms from Communication Focus 4 to express different thoughts you have.

   Example: Clearly, what Mr. Brooke did was . . .

How Anonymous Are You Online?

Peace River resident Richard Brooke was fired yesterday for posting comments critical of the local government that he works for. Mr. Brooke wrote seven or eight anonymous posts for the *Coffee News*, an online journal, attacking the Peace River Town Council. Mr. Brooke is employed by the Town of Peace River's municipal tax office. Although Brooke's postings were anonymous and *Coffee News* guarantees anonymity, *Coffee News* reporter Debbie Farris discovered that the commenter writing the attacks under the name "Peace Lover," was Mr. Brooke, a government employee, and matched him with his alias. Farris wrote an article the next day highlighting Mr. Brooke's attacks on his own employer. The article was read by Peace River mayor Louis Venton, who fired Brooke immediately.

Mr. Brooke is very upset that the *Coffee News* has broken its promise of respecting anonymity.

SPEAKING ACTIVITY 14

Asking *Why?* repeatedly may seem annoying, but it is a great way to dig deeply into the root issue and find a possible solution to a problem. Decide on a possible problem from the list below. Practise asking four complete *Why?* questions that build on the information each time and see if you can find the root problem and a solution to it.

Example:

Person A: <u>My brand new cell phone has a broken screen.</u> (Problem)

Person B: **(1) Why does your new cell phone have a broken screen?**

Person A: **Because I dropped my phone on the ground and it landed on its corner.**

Person B: **(2) Why did you drop it?**

Person A: **I dropped it while I was searching through my purse for a stick of gum.**

Person B: **(3) Why were you holding the phone at the same time as you were searching through your purse?**

Person A: **I didn't want to put my new phone on the ground, and I had no other place to put it.**

Person B: **(4) Why . . .**

Possible problems:

1. I wasn't able to finish my homework that is due today.
2. I tried to speak with my family back home on VoIP, but it didn't work.
3. Jun's parents wanted to move to Hawaii last year, but it wasn't possible.
4. I wanted to go to a concert with five of my friends, but it didn't work out.
5. Other (Make your own.)

🚶🚶 SPEAKING ACTIVITY 15

With your partner, analyze the posters below. Talk about your knowledge of IBM and "smart technologies" or "smart cities." List the specifics of what is actually there in each of the posters. Identify the intent and the message of each ad. Finally, discuss your impressions of the ad campaign including your analysis and judgment.

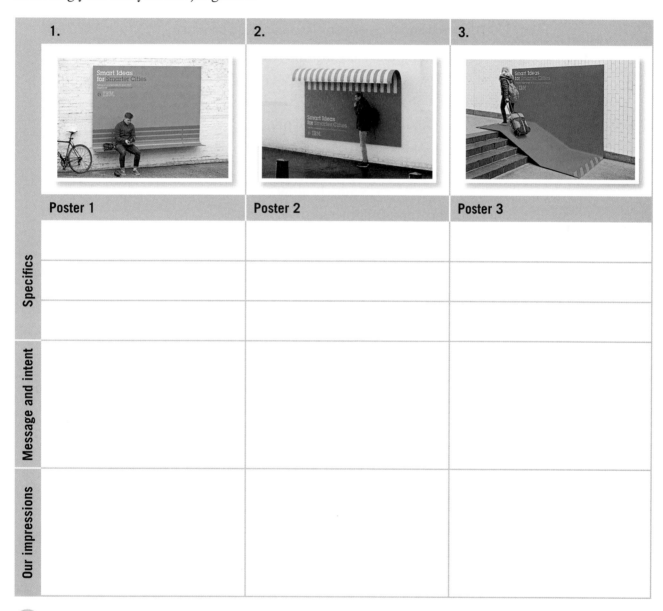

	Poster 1	Poster 2	Poster 3
Specifics			
Message and intent			
Our impressions			

🚶🚶 SPEAKING ACTIVITY 16

Individually, create notes for a two-minute impromptu speech on one of the following four topics. With a partner, take turns delivering your speeches to each other.

The Pros and Cons of Facebook   The Reliability of Web Information

The Internet as a Communication   Sharing of Personal Information
Facilitator

After you listen to your partner's mini-speech, organize an analysis on it, then deliver a brief one-minute review to him or her.

When organizing an analysis for presentation, follow these four steps:

1. Give background information about the topic.
2. Organize the information (give pros and cons, ranking, process, etc.).
3. Express your analysis of the data using language you have learned in Communication Focus 4.
4. Highlight key takeaways for listeners.

👥 **SPEAKING ACTIVITY 17**

Work with your partner to organize lists of each of the following:

Examples:

a ranking of the most commonly used words in English

> **Most commonly used words in English: 1.** *the*; **2.** *and*; **3.** *of*; **4** . . .

the pros and cons of your favourite web browser

> **Safari: Pros**—very fast, reliable . . . **Cons**—doesn't work well with Java . . .

1. the pros and cons of electric cars
2. a ranking of the best cell phones
3. a ranking of the best cars
4. the steps in learning a language
5. the steps to living a healthy life
6. the steps in a process

Example:

> **Making coffee**—First, grind coffee beans, then run hot water through the grounds. Next, . . .

👥 **SPEAKING ACTIVITY 18**

A. Working in pairs, you will first analyze some data. Choose one of the four following sources of data about social media usage and practices. Follow the steps outlined in the speaking strategy on this page and prepare a two- to three-minute analysis.

B. Together, articulate your analysis to your group.

1. Social Media Usage

Which of the Following Social Media Do You Use?

Facebook
YouTube
Twitter
Google+
LinkedIn
Pinterest
MySpace
Instagram
Tumblr
Foursquare

■ 2012
■ 2011

0%   20%   40%   60%   80%   100%

2. Social Media Types

3. Social Media Policy

4. Social Media Popularity by Country

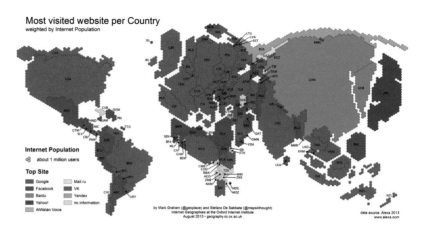

PRONUNCIATION

Pronunciation Focus 1: Reducing Vowel Sounds

In natural speech, vowel sounds are often reduced to the sound / ə /, called schwa. It's one of the middle vowel sounds. While content words are spoken clearly and stressed, unstressed syllables and grammatical function words such as *can*, *of*, *and*, *to*, and *or* are reduced.

 Track 27

 PRONUNCIATION ACTIVITY 1

Listen to the words and sentences and repeat after each. Note how the underlined vowel sounds are reduced.

Steven	Amelia	photographs	should've
a problem	Susan	Edmonton	Regina
remember	Canada	some	
asleep	licence	lessons	

1. She can drive a car.
2. He's taking some photographs.
3. I'd love to go to South America.
4. It's a quarter to eleven.

Track 28

PRONUNCIATION ACTIVITY 2

A. Listen to the dialogue about Amelia. Note how the underlined vowel sounds are reduced.

Dialogue:

Steven: Amelia has a problem. She wants to go to Regina, but I don't think she drives.

Susan: Well, she drives—she took some lessons, but she didn't get a licence.

Steven: Yeah, she would've passed, but the day of the test, she fell asleep in the test centre.

Susan: I remember. They waited, but Amelia missed it.

Steven: We should've taken some photographs.

Susan: So she'll take the bus to Edmonton, and probably fly from there.

Steven: Probably. I hope she remembers to bring her passport.

Susan: Yeah, or some kind of official ID.

B. Practise reading the dialogue aloud with a partner.

PRONUNCIATION ACTIVITY 3

Reduced form for *can* and *can't*

Track 29

Sometimes we use long *can* / kæn /, and sometimes we use reduced *can* / kən /. The vowel in *can't* (/ kænt /) is not reduced.

A. Listen to the dialogue about personal skills.

Person A: I can **swim**. I can **skate**. I **can't** ski.

Person B: Can you **sing**?

Person A: No, I **can't**, but I can **dance**.

Person B: Let me show you my special skill.

I can **catch** 25 coins off my elbow.

Do you think I **can**?

Person A: Yes I think you **can**.

B. Practise making impromptu dialogues comparing your abilities with your partner's. Use *can* and *can't*.

PRONUNCIATION ACTIVITY 4

Reduced form for *of*

Sometimes *of* sounds like a schwa sound.

Example: a flock of birds → a flock / ə / birds

Work with your partner to match the amounts in the left column with the items in the right.

a(n) + amount (noun) + *of* + thing (noun)

Practise saying the combinations below. When you're finished, use the photo for ideas as you add your own examples to the list.

Example:

> **a bag of chips** sounds like **a bag o' /ə/ chips**

a pad of	butter
a box of	flowers
a tube of	whipped cream
300 grams of	beer
a bar of	paper
a can of	chocolates
a carton of	toothpaste
a six-pack of	soap
a bag of	milk
a bouquet of	chips

_____ _____ _____ _____

_____ _____ _____ _____

👥 PRONUNCIATION ACTIVITY 5

Fixed phrases with reduced *and*

Sometimes *and* is reduced to simply the sound / ən /.

Example: ham and eggs → ham n eggs

A. Practise saying these possible names for fast food stands. Notice that *and* has been reduced to '*n*'.

Fish 'n' Chips   Stop 'n' Go   Sweet 'n' Sour   Meat 'n' Potatoes

Franks 'n' Beans   Eat 'n' Run

B. Discuss in what contexts you would use those sample names. Have a chat with your partner to choose a good name for a food stand in your school cafeteria.

👥 PRONUNCIATION ACTIVITY 6

Reduced forms for *to*

Usually, *to* / tu / is reduced to / tə /.

A. Practise the following backward buildup drill. As you say each line, swing your arm once (one beat). Keep practising until you can say Line 1 and Line 3 in the same beat.

Line 1	store
Line 2	the store
Line 3	to the store (say *to* as / tə /)

B. Practise sharing directions to local sites with your partner. Use the following expressions:

to get to the . . .

turn to the left at . . .   turn to the right at . . .

to the corner of . . .

go to the . . .   go up/down X street to the corner of . . .

👥 PRONUNCIATION ACTIVITY 7

Fixed phrases with reduced *or*

Work with a partner to supply the missing words in the following sentences.

1. You keep leaving the house and then coming back; are you in or _____?

2. Which one do you want, this or _____?

3. I don't know whose it is, but it's either his or _____.

4. Is this elevator going up or _____?

5. You look confused; are you coming or _____?

6. I can't find the map; should we turn left or _____?

7. Win or _____, I've been a Stampeders fan for 20 years.

8. It looks like the test won't be for two or _____ weeks.

Pronunciation Focus 2: Recognizing Syllables

🎧 **Track 30**

Syllables are the building blocks of words. In English, being able to recognize them is linked to the study of spelling, vocabulary, and pronunciation. Every syllable has one vowel sound.

Examples:

bought (two vowels, but one vowel sound)

neighbourhood (six vowels, but three vowel sounds)

👥 PRONUNCIATION ACTIVITY 8

Work with your partner to count the number of syllables in each word. Note that the number of vowels may differ from the number of vowel sounds. Listen and repeat to check your answers.

forum	____	precedent	____
spectrum	____	perplex	____
intriguing	____	devastating	____
prompt	____	brainwashed	____
authentic	____	counterintuitive	____
deteriorate	____	resolve	____

🞉 PRONUNCIATION ACTIVITY 9

A haiku poem consists of three lines about one topic. The first and last lines have five syllables, and the middle line has seven syllables. Find and circle each syllable in the following haiku poems and then practise saying them (the number of syllables is given in parentheses).

Next, write your own haiku poem and recite it to the class.

Haiku 1	Haiku 2	Your Haiku
Boys and girls skating (5) Canada's sport unites all (7) Family and dear friends (5)	I walk across snow (5) Thinking about the summer (7) When will it return (5)	

Pronunciation Focus 3: Recognizing Syllable Stress

Although a dictionary is the best source to confirm which syllables are stressed, there are some rules of thumb.

1. In many two-syllable <u>nouns</u> the stress is on the first syllable.

   present, export, classroom

2. In many two-syllable <u>verbs</u> where the second syllable has a diphthong or long vowel, the second syllable is stressed.

   proceed, constrain, exclude, decide

3. Certain suffixes are usually stressed: *-ese, -ette, -ee*.

   Chinese, cigarette, nominee

4. Certain suffixes push the stress back one syllable earlier: *-ic, -tion, -sion, -graphy, -ive, -logy*.

   gigantic, action, fiction, television, photography, biography, active, creative, biology, ecology

🞉 PRONUNCIATION ACTIVITY 10

A. Practise saying the words below by placing stress on the first syllable for nouns and on the second syllable for verbs. Then, make sentences with them.

Example:

ínsert (noun)	The magazine had a colour insert full of advertising.
insért (verb)	Naji had to insert his credit card to pay the bill.

export	record	recall	address
produce	subject	insult	conduct
project	suspect	object	present

B. Use your dictionary as necessary to help you understand the meaning and usage of the following items. Then, make sentences with them.

Example:

dropout (noun)   Alfonso is a high school dropout.

drop out (verb)   A 16-year old may legally drop out of school, but it is not considered a good idea.

ripoff	rip off	situp	sit up
workout	work out	takeoff	take off
takeout	take out		

PRONUNCIATION ACTIVITY 11

Referring to the guidelines in Pronunciation Focuses 2 and 3, work with your partner to place stress marks above the stressed syllables in the following words. You may use a dictionary as necessary. When you have finished, check the answers with your teacher. Then, make a short story with your partner using as many of the words as you can. Take turns telling your story to other pairs.

Example:

resolve

historic   mountain   voyage   romance   story   action   decide

include   avoid   picture   authentic   transcend   perplex   constrain

Pronunciation Focus 4: Applying Syllable Stress

 Track 31   **Stressed** syllables have either longer vowel sounds or higher pitch, while **unstressed** syllables are shorter and softer, and have reduced vowel sounds. Listen to and repeat the six words. Be careful to copy the same stress pattern as you hear.

Stress Patterns (O = stressed; • = unstressed)					
O •	**• O**	**• O •**	**O • •**	**• • O**	**O • • •**
doctor	consent	elective	vegetable	engineer	calculator

PRONUNCIATION ACTIVITY 12

Work with a partner to distribute the words below among the columns with words of the same stress pattern in the chart on the next page. As you do the exercise, practise saying all the words out loud. When you are not sure where the main stress falls, ask your teacher or consult a dictionary.

alter	understand	request	forum	exam
employment	calculator	essential	spectrum	insist
annual	authentic	alphabet	circumstances	media

Stress Patterns (O = stressed, • = unstressed)					
O •	• O	• O •	O • •	• • O	O • • •

👤👤👤 PRONUNCIATION ACTIVITY 13

Work with your group to write in the chart and practise saying as many of your own words as you can that follow the indicated stress patterns. Check your answers with your teacher.

Group A: animals; Group B: food and drink; Group C verbs; Group D: people's names

Stress Patterns (O = stressed, • = unstressed)					
O •	• O	• O •	O • •	• • O	O • • •

COMMUNICATING IN THE REAL WORLD

Working with a partner, create a survey of eight questions inquiring how the Internet is changing languages. Six of the questions should be closed and two open. Write your questions on one sheet of paper for easy reference, then prepare a brief greeting to introduce yourself to interviewees. Show the questions and introduction to the teacher for accuracy. Practise introducing yourself and asking your questions with a friend. When you are ready, introduce yourself and ask your questions of five native speakers of English. Audio-record interviewees' responses, so you can listen and take careful notes of each of the responses in the outline on the next page.

Question Board Topic:
Q1 (closed):
Q2 (closed):
Q3 (closed):
Q4 (closed):
Q5 (closed):
Q6 (closed):
Q7 (open):
Q8 (open):

Notes			
Interviewees	**Responses**		
Speaker #1	Q1:	Q2:	Q3:
	Q4:	Q5:	Q6:
	Q7:		
	Q8:		
Speaker #2	Q1:	Q2:	Q3:
	Q4:	Q5:	Q6:
	Q7:		
	Q8:		
Speaker #3	Q1:	Q2:	Q3:
	Q4:	Q5:	Q6:
	Q7:		
	Q8:		
Speaker #4	Q1:	Q2:	Q3:
	Q4:	Q5:	Q6:
	Q7:		
	Q8:		
Speaker #5	Q1:	Q2:	Q3:
	Q4:	Q5:	Q6:
	Q7:		
	Q8:		

After you have completed your notes, express an analysis of your findings to your classmates by comparing each of the responses for all questions and summarizing what you learned from this.

SELF-EVALUATION

Think about your work in this chapter. For each row in the chart sections **Grammar and Language Functions**, **Pronunciation**, **Learning Strategies**, and **Note-Taking**, give yourself a score based on the rating scale below and write a comment in the Notes section.

Show the chart to your teacher. Talk about what you need to do to make your English better.

Rating Scale

1	2	3	4	5

Needs ⟵─────────────────────⟶ *Great!*
improvement.

	Score	Notes
Grammar and Language Functions		
asking questions to gather information		
using interrogatives		
summarizing information		
paraphrasing information		
using reported speech		
expressing an analysis		
Pronunciation		
reducing vowel sounds to schwa		
recognizing syllables		
recognizing syllable stress		
applying syllable stress		
Learning Strategies		
Speaking		
rephrasing to facilitate communication		
organizing an analysis for presentation		
Listening		
making a pre-listening plan		
synthesizing new information with prior knowledge to remember details more easily		

Note-Taking		
using symbols, short forms, and abbreviations		
organizing a narrative chronologically		

Vocabulary and Language Chunks

Look at this list of new vocabulary and language chunks you learned in this chapter. Give yourself a score based on the rating scale and write a comment.

precedent	essentially	acknowledge	an expanding array
degeneration	deteriorate	disengage	of . . .
dialect	alter	graduate school	the motivation
perception	constrain	relocation	behind . . .
forum	prompt	Skype/Twitter	you can't assume
spectrum	CD	perplex	that . . .
counterintuitive	concentrated	transcend	make generalizations
renowned	proximity to	authentic	about . . .
brainwashed	resolve	a good example is . . .	to have a point
devastating	exclusive	to a considerable	to engage with
expressive	constraints of	extent	to immerse oneself in
intriguing		has a _____ (adj.)	to log on
		dimension	to make do
		is predominantly	to strike up a
		(written)	conversation
		the novelty of . . .	

	Score	Notes
understanding new vocabulary and language chunks		
using new lexical items freely and confidently		

My plan for practising is _____

_____

_____

_____

CHAPTER 3

Humans and Technology

Making inferences

Using discourse markers

Supporting a proposition with infographics

THINKING AND TALKING

Humans and technology are increasingly intertwined, and life without the Internet is increasingly unavoidable, if not difficult to think about, for many. This pairing of technology and humanity isn't always considered safe, however.

Look at the pictures below. What do you think the relationships are between the people and the technology? Do you see any potential for negative aspects?

LISTENING 1

Before You Listen

PRE-LISTENING ACTIVITY 1

Information is being recorded about you all the time through your phone calls, emails, texts, search history, online purchases, in-store purchases, contacts, friends, and places you go.

In small groups, consider these questions:

> What examples are there of people or organizations gathering information about you? Who is gathering this information? What is done with this information? Is it being gathered for security purposes? What are some other reasons information about you is being tracked and saved?

PRE-LISTENING ACTIVITY 2

Every day, people agree to long legal agreements without giving them much thought. Social networking sites, iTunes, and email providers all offer terms and conditions that potential users must agree to in order to be allowed access. Discuss these two questions with a partner:

1. Have you ever agreed to terms and conditions online without reading all the details? Why? Which companies did you do this for?
2. What do you think those legal terms and conditions might involve?

UPFRONT VOCABULARY

NSA	National Security Agency, USA
CSEC [sea-sek]	Communications Security Establishment Canada
Snowden, Edward	former employee of the CIA, known for revealing secret information
revelations	normally hidden facts that people are suddenly made aware of
legalistic	obeying the law too strictly*
jargon	specialized language used in a certain field or profession
scam	a clever and dishonest plan for making money*
sham	a system that is not as good or true as it seems to be*
surveillance	systematic observation

*Definition courtesy of *Oxford Advanced Learner's Dictionary.*

PRE-LISTENING VOCABULARY

Discuss the synonyms in the chart with a partner to help you understand the meaning of the new vocabulary. Then, work together to complete the sentences with the correct vocabulary.

Vocabulary	**Synonyms**
ultimately	eventually, finally
anticipate	expect, await, predict
antiquated	old-fashioned, obsolete, out-dated, archaic
augment	supplement, expand, enhance
enticing	tempting, alluring, inviting, appealing
up in arms	angry, irate
legislation	law, rule, regulation
public sector	government controlled, taxpayer funded

1. The typewriter is a good example of an _____ technology.

2. I am certain that technology will _____ have more benefits than drawbacks.

3. Technology has the ability to _____ progress.

4. The girl in the picture is _____ about her friend's behaviour.

5. Reading the legal agreements on websites isn't _____ for most people.

6. CSEC employees are part of the _____ of Canada.

7. For most people it is difficult to _____ what the next technological invention will be.

8. Technological innovation is happening so quickly, it is difficult for _____ to keep up.

Note-Taking

 **Track 32**

In this segment of a show from the CBC Radio program *Spark*, host Nora Young and Kevin Haggerty, a professor of sociology and criminology at the University of Alberta, discuss the importance of surveillance and the impact that surveillance has on society.

Taking notes is not an exercise in transcribing everything being said, but a way for you to remember the most important parts of it. As you listen to the interview for the first time, don't write out entire questions and answers. Instead, focus on the questions, and take notes by writing a word or two with a question mark for each question asked by the interviewer. Also, write only one- or two-word answers.

Questions	**Answers**
1. who H.?	U of Alb. Prof, Soc. & Crim.
2. specialty?	_____
3. _____	_____
	_____
	_____
	_____
	_____
4. _____	_____
	_____
	_____
	_____
5. _____	_____

Listening for the Main Ideas

 **Track 33**

A. Listen to the interview again and expand on your notes from the previous activity. Then, use your notes to answer the questions.

B. When you are finished, compare your answers with those of a classmate. Be ready to explain your answers.

 **Listening STRATEGY**

Critical listening involves recognizing and understanding a speaker's point of view (POV), or bias. Always consider whether or not your own bias affects your understanding.

1. What is Kevin Haggerty's specialty?

2. What's the difference between how most people feel about surveillance and how Kevin feels about it?

3. What does Kevin explain about how surveillance cameras are changing?

4. How does Kevin feel about laws regarding surveillance that should protect people?

5. Why does he say this is so?

6. Kevin explains that consent is a sham. Why does he think this?

7. What is the problem with the privacy laws?

Listening Comprehension

 **Track 34**

A. Listen to each excerpt from the interview. Pause as necessary and write exactly what you hear, then answer the question about that excerpt. Answer each question before transcribing the next excerpt.

Excerpt 1:

Transcribe: I think actually _____

_____

What does Kevin assume to be true regarding most people's knowledge of surveillance?

Answer: _____

_____

Excerpt 2:

Transcribe: From 200 metres away _____

_____

What can you assume from this information about using your smartphone in public?

Answer: _____

_____

Excerpt 3:

Transcribe: Camera infrastructure is _____

_____

What does Kevin mean to tell us with this information?

Answer: _____

_____

Excerpt 4:

Transcribe: I don't think that _____

_____

What do you understand from this statement?

Answer: _____

_____

B. When you have finished the activity, compare your answers with those of a partner. Try to explain your reasons for your answers, and decide what you think the intended message of each sentence is.

Listening **STRATEGY**

Ask yourself which content points support or contradict the validity of the speaker's bias by:

1. **determining if there is bias:** ask if there is a balance of information from both sides presented

2. **identifying aspects of the bias:** listen for facts versus opinions

Personalizing

A. Have any of these things ever happened to you? Discuss the following situations with a partner.

1. You bought something online and when it arrived, it was not what you had expected.
2. You ordered something off the menu at a restaurant and were surprised by what you received.
3. You went on a blind date and your date was different from what you had hoped.
4. You registered for a course and the content was not what you had anticipated.
5. You signed up for a lecture that had a misleading title.
6. You agreed to do something with a friend and had completely different ideas about what was agreed on.

B. Think of one of your own examples of mistaken expectations and share it with your partner.

Vocabulary and Language Chunks

A. Match the following language chunks with their definitions, then, with a partner, make sentences with as many new language chunks as you can.

Language Chunks	**Meanings**
1. caring capacity	____ the basis of how sth happens or works
2. blurring of boundaries	____ began and is still ongoing
3. the nature of (surveillance)	____ non-government business
4. private sector	____ a person's ability to be thoughtful, kind, or considerate
5. started out	____ when limitations or restrictions become unclear
6. it tells us	____ we understand

B. Work with a partner and think of as many synonyms as you can for each of the following vocabulary items. Use your dictionary, thesaurus, or word processor to help you, if available.

Vocabulary	Synonyms
capacity	*volume, size, bulk; ability*
infrared	
infrastructure	
adequate	
consent	
reactive	
sufficient	
underfunded	

SPEAKING 1

Communication Focus 1: Making Inferences

An inference is a logical conclusion based on input, usually data or prior knowledge. Making inferences is an important step in the scientific process. There are two basic kinds of inferences. Sometimes the input for the inference is simply factual data. But sometimes the input includes something that is assumed (based on incomplete or incorrect data) to be true (but may not be). This second kind may therefore lead to mistaken conclusions.

data (what we know)　➔　**a (fact-based) inference**

data (what we know) + **assumption**　➔　**a (partially fact-based) inference**

Examples:

(We know) **It is winter.**　➔　**It is not summer.** (fact-based) inference

(We know) **It is winter.**

+ Assumption: **Winter is always cold.**　➔　**It must be cold today.** (partially fact-based) inference

The partially fact-based inference may or may not be true, as it could be a warm day.

Grammar Note: Modals

Modals are helping verbs that express properties such as ability, obligation, possibility, and probability.

The modal *must* is often used to show inference.

Examples:

She is not wearing a gold ring on her ring finger.　➔　She <u>must</u> not be married.

He is wearing a gold ring on his finger.　➔　He <u>must</u> like wearing a gold ring.

▲▲▲ SPEAKING ACTIVITY 1

Work with group mates to make inferences based on the following criteria using the modal *must*.

Example:

Data	The teacher is wearing a red shirt.
Inferences	The shirt must belong to the teacher.
	The teacher must have bought the red shirt.
	The teacher mustn't like other colours.
	The teacher must always wear red.

Data

1. Your friend is not in class today.

2. One of your classmates is wearing a ring.

3. Your classmate's mother has a full-time job and is attending night school.

4. You have been calling your friend since 8:00 PM but no one is answering.

5. You see a student having lunch in the cafeteria alone.

6. A friend of the opposite sex asks you to dinner.

7. One of your friends doesn't eat meat.

8. Your best friend in your class received a much higher grade on a test than you did.

9. Grandfather always asks you to repeat what you say.

👥 SPEAKING ACTIVITY 2

Work in small groups to list as many inferences as you can about the pictures. Compare your lists with the whole class and discuss whether the inferences are believable.

👥 SPEAKING ACTIVITY 3

Inferences can be inaccurate and sometimes can offend others. As you do the following exercise, pay attention to the nuances of cultural sensitivities. Working in small groups, observe your group mates and state facts and possible inferences about them based on the following categories. Remember, your inferences may be incorrect, so check if you are right by asking your group mates.

When you have finished, discuss the different reactions to statements of fact and inferences.

1. shirt colour

2. first language

3. ethnicity

4. brand of smartphone

5. age

👥 **SPEAKING ACTIVITY 4**

Work with a partner and decide what the inference is in each of the following statements, then restate them, eliminating the uncertainty.

Example:

Statement: **A student applying for financial aid should submit her application by Friday.**

Inference: **The students are all female.**

Restated: **Students applying for financial aid should submit applications by Friday.**

Statement: Policemen in our city are polite and completely trustworthy.

Inference:

Restated:

Statement: They are speaking another language; I wonder what country they are from.

Inference:

Restated:

Statement: My friend drives like a farmer.

Inference:

Restated:

Statement: I love philosophy—it is our most interesting class.

Inference:

Restated:

Statement: Are you sure you should eat a fourth cookie?

Inference:

Restated:

Statement: I left five bucks in the cup of a guy asleep on a park bench.

Inference:

Restated:

Statement: Are there always so many foreigners in this café?

Inference:

Restated:

👥 SPEAKING ACTIVITY 5

In the following activity, try to separate the facts from the inferences. Read the story and work with your partner to label the statements about the story.

True (**T**) = 100 percent true and factual

False (**F**) = 100 percent false

? = It could be true or it could be false. (It is not absolutely true or absolutely false.)

> **The Story**
>
> A businessman had just turned off the lights in the store when a man appeared and demanded money. The owner opened a cash register. The contents of the cash register were scooped up and the man sped away. A member of the police force was contacted promptly.
>
> (Source: Excerpted from "The Uncritical Inference Test," in *Communication and Organizational Behaviour*, 3rd edition by William V. Haney.)

Statements about the Story

1. A man appeared after the owner had turned off his store lights. ____
2. The robber was a man. ____
3. The man who appeared did not demand money. ____
4. The man who opened the cash register was the owner. ____
5. The store owner scooped up the contents of the cash register and ran away. ____
6. Someone opened a cash register. ____
7. The cash register contained money. ____
8. After the store lights were turned off a man appeared. ____
9. Taking the contents of the cash register with him, the man ran out of the store. ____
10. The story involves four people: the businessman, the store owner, a man who appeared and demanded money, and a member of the police force. ____

(Source: Statements adapted from "The Uncritical Inference Test," in *Communication and Organizational Behaviour*, 3rd edition by William V. Haney.)

After you have been provided with the answers, analyze your mistakes with your partner.

👥 SPEAKING ACTIVITY 6

Recognizing the difference between fact and opinion is a vital critical thinking skill. While inferences may originate from factual information, opinions are not necessarily based on evidence at all, and are not part of the scientific process. If you want to express ideas and opinions that cannot be supported with facts, begin with expressions like these:

> In my view, . . .
>
> It is my view that . . .
>
> It seems to me that . . .
>
> As far as I'm concerned, . . .
>
> From the point of view of . . .
>
> In the opinion of . . .

Alternate with your partner reading the following sentences. The listening partner states if the sentence is fact or opinion and explains why.

Example:

> Some Canadian municipal police forces use drones (Unmanned Aerial Vehicles) to assist police investigations.
>
> Fact ✔ Opinion ___
>
> Explanation: It is verifiable with a fact. The Halton Police Force (Ontario), for example, started a drone program in 2009.

1. Data monitoring records changes users make to files on a computer's hard drive.

   Fact ___ Opinion ___

   Explanation:

2. Keystroke logging records all keyboard input a user has typed or entered on a computer.

   Fact ___ Opinion ___

   Explanation:

3. School administrators and teachers need to monitor student computer usage.

   Fact ___ Opinion ___

   Explanation:

4. Post-secondary institutions in Canada should monitor student online activity including email.

   Fact ___ Opinion ___

   Explanation:

5. Screen monitoring, data monitoring, and keystroke logging are all types of surveillance.

   Fact ___ Opinion ___

   Explanation:

Speaking STRATEGY

Avoid stating opinions as if they are facts, because discussions and logical arguments will fall apart if you do. Healthy discussions occur when opinions are expressed or identified as what they are: opinions.

👥 SPEAKING ACTIVITY 7

Work with a partner to complete the following table. When you have finished, share your answers with your class.

Fact (can be proven)	Inference (based on fact)	Opinion
Class starts at 8:30.	If I arrive after 8:30, I will be considered late.	Nobody cares if I show up after 8:30.
		Our language lab is too small.
	The Internet is down on campus.	
The lab has 28 computers.		
	Somebody else has been using this desk.	
		Flying is more dangerous than driving.

LISTENING 2

Before You Listen

👥 PRE-LISTENING ACTIVITY 1

Good shoppers need also to be good online researchers. Imagine you and your partner are shopping on a tech gadgets website. Make a list of the product categories you would expect to see there. For example, your list of categories may include bags, cameras, computer accessories, etc.

👥👥 PRE-LISTENING ACTIVITY 2

Review the list of categories you created in the previous activity. Call out one of the categories and give your group mates 90 seconds to list as many examples of gadgets within that category as possible.

Example:

    Computer accessories: speakers, SIM card, microphone . . .

Repeat with the other categories on your list.

Activity Extension 1. Change the theme of your categories to an area other than tech gadgets, for example, professions (lawyer, doctor, etc.); dance styles (waltz, hip hop, jazz, etc.); teacher talk ("Okay class, open your books."); and so on.

Activity Extension 2. Reverse the process. List examples from within one category while your group mates guess which category you are listing for.

Example:

> "Windows, aquariums, mirrors, . . ."   "Things made of glass!"

UPFRONT VOCABULARY

techblog	a technical online diary or journal
gear	equipment or clothing needed for a particular activity: climbing/fishing/sports, etc.*
gadget	a small tool or device that does sth useful*
novelty	the quality of being new, different, and interesting*
materialism	a belief that money, possessions, and physical comforts are more important than values*
metrics	relating to or involving measurement

*Definition courtesy of *Oxford Advanced Learner's Dictionary*.

PRE-LISTENING VOCABULARY

A. Work with a partner and match the following words with their synonyms. Use a dictionary as necessary.

Key Words	Synonyms
1. write-up	____ guidelines, indications
2. trade show	____ branch, partner
3. specs	____ repetition, uniformity
4. sameness	____ account, report
5. affiliate	____ display, exposition

B. Work with a partner to think of as many verb–noun collocations as you can with the nouns in the list.

Nouns	Verbs
sameness (n)	recognize, observe, require, demand, achieve
write-up (n)	_____
trade show (n)	_____
specs (n)	_____
affiliate (n)	_____

Note-Taking

Do you need a water bottle? How about a fitness tracker or a new printer? Do you need those? Do you want the best one for the price? Brian Lam has created a website called *The Wirecutter*, which is based on extensively researched "best of" lists of technology. In this CBC interview, Brian describes how his team of writers test products and determine the best of each kind so that you don't have to.

 Track 35

Good notes express a visual system of organization that shows main ideas and supporting details by linking each detail to the main idea it supports. Create a diagram like the relationship graphic pictured, then listen to the interview and fill in the main ideas and the supporting details.

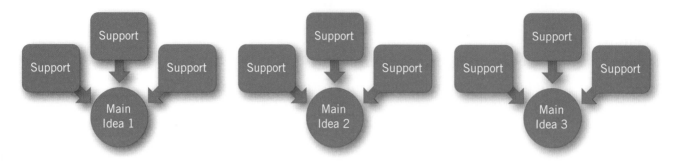

Listening for the Main Ideas

 Track 36

A. Listen to the interview with Brian Lam again and add to your notes.

B. Use your notes to help you discuss the following six ideas with your partner and rank them in order of significance to the main message of the audio. When you've finished, check your answers with the rest of the class.

____ Gizmodo got away from their original ideas about providing service.

____ One article a week (low volume) is better than too much content.

____ Brian recognizes the importance of his contract with his readers.

____ Brian's website helps relieve the stress and anxiety of selecting the best gadgets.

____ It is dangerous to focus too much on novelty; we need to overcome materialism.

 Listening STRATEGY

Recognize the speaker's priorities by determining which idea or ideas relate most closely to the thesis of the talk. This listening strategy will help you organize your notes.

Listening Comprehension

 Track 37

Listen to the interview with Brian Lam again and write down examples that he gives for each of the following:

1. gadget categories

_____

2. metrics

_____

3. the features of Brian's business model

_____

4. what Brian's contract with his readers encourages them to do

_____

5. the mind games Brian plays with himself

_____

Personalizing

Work with your partner to make lists of features that would appeal to you if you were going to buy these items. Discuss why these features are important to you.

smartphone	brand, weight, size, features, display, . . .
tablet	_____
laptop	_____
car	_____
pair of shoes	_____
other: _____	_____

Vocabulary and Language Chunks

Some language chunks from the audio are used in context in the sentences below to help you better understand what they mean and how they are used. Read the sentences, then work with your partner to match each expression with its usage.

1. They do that because their **business model** depends on it.
2. His team of writers will try out products and **wade through the sea of** online reviews so you don't have to.
3. **It's all about getting** more page views and more traffic so you can sell more ads.
4. **My gut always told** me it wasn't healthy and people just didn't want to see that much content.
5. Brian says that the tech media's **thirst for** website traffic etc. has led to a kind of sameness.
6. There's no **conflict of interest** because . . . we make no money . . . we don't get an affiliate fee.
7. This is **the right call**, because it is dangerous to get into this position of recommending products.
8. If you have a hobby that's an **all-consuming** passion, you wanna get the best stuff.
9. I **play** all these **mind games** to make sure that I'm being correct in my thinking.

Language Chunks	Meanings
1. business model	____ mostly concerning or focused on a certain topic
2. wade through a sea of	____ use psychological tactics
3. it's all about	____ struggle to find one among very many
4. my gut tells me	____ intense
5. a thirst for sth	____ I have a sense or strong feeling
6. a conflict of interest	____ an unfair advantage gained through a favourable position

7. the right call   ____ an organization's illustration of its
                                  strategic plan

8. all-consuming   ____ the best/correct decision

9. play mind games   ____ a desperate need

SPEAKING 2

Communication Focus 2: Using Discourse Markers

Language is dynamic and people organize what they say in different ways. In a conversation, discourse markers help the listener understand what is being said in relation to what was said before and what will follow. A speaker's ability to use discourse markers accurately and appropriately shows a higher level of language comprehension and language production on that speaker's part.

This is a chart of some of the many discourse markers that speakers commonly use. This is not a complete list, so add other discourse markers to this list when you learn them.

Function Category	Language Function	Discourse Marker
1. To indicate the start or end of speaking	start	I'd like to say/ask . . . so/now/okay/right, . . . (Today) I'm going to talk about . . .
	end (conclude)	in conclusion, finally, in summary, to wrap up (These may be used with a drop in pitch or loudness.)
2. To aid a speaker in controlling a conversation	hold the floor	but, and, however, like
	fill time, hesitate	uhm, er, you know, it's like. . . (Note: Fillers are often followed by interruptions by the listener.)
	change topics	anyway, by the way, moving on . . .
3. To introduce information	explain why	because, since, as, due to . . .
	clarify/focus	actually, I mean, in other words, basically, you see, certainly
	generalize	I'd guess, about, around, basically
	exemplify	say, such as, like, for example
	expand	additionally, another thing is, besides that
	contrast	on the other hand, although, you'd think that, even though, however, otherwise
	state a result	therefore, so, as a result, consequently
	sequence	then, next, before/after that, later, previously, meanwhile, at the same time, consecutively
	summarize	to make a long story short, in summary, in conclusion, essentially

Function Category	Language Function	Discourse Marker
4. To make dialogues flow more easily	emphasize	above all, . . . is really important, as a matter of fact, certainly, in fact, actually, what could be more natural than to . . .
	state a circumstance	presumably, when, as, after, since, once, until, while, supposedly
	make a concession	but, although, however, yet, though, still
	indicate conditions	in that case, then, if that's true

🏃 SPEAKING ACTIVITY 8

Think about what the speakers below are *doing with the language* (as opposed to what they are *saying*). Work with your partner and discuss what the functions are of the underlined discourse markers in the sentences below. The sentences are from the interview with Brian Lam.

Note: Not all the discourse markers used here are defined above, so discuss with your partner which of the four types these markers might be.

Nora: Like, say you're here, in a typical electronics store. You're here because you're looking for something specific, say, a new TV.

Nora: Basically, thewirecutter.com is a list.

Brian: Essentially, everyone is trying to print money.

Brian: I don't know if that's a good use of anyone's time. I mean, I certainly don't want to use my time as a journalist in front of my computer writing about other peoples' work all the time.

Nora: I mean a lot of online writing is supported by advertising—and often that means the writing is formatted around page views.

Brian: You'd think that over time we would've found a way to differentiate between those pages and those pages.

Nora: Because, presumably, Amazon doesn't care whether you buy gadget X or gadget Y from them.

Brian: I definitely think it's a dangerous thing to get obsessed with novelty.

Brian: Like, it's really important to realize that you can get the job done with older tools.

Brian: And $2,000 dollars is, like, a dive trip to some tropical place. You know, it's like Wow! Maybe I can keep my computer for another year.

Brian: But, you know, the reason why I did this site is, uhm, is because I needed to make a living.

Brian: And, so, uhm, that's how I live with myself, actually.

👥 SPEAKING ACTIVITY 9

Each of these groups of expressions has a language function. Discuss what these expressions do, and then make sentences that express that function.

Example:

Group A:

In conclusion, . . .

In summary, . . .

Finally, . . .

Function: These expressions indicate the end of someone's talk.

Group B:

The reason why . . .

It is because . . .

So . . .

Function: _____

Group C:

For example, . . .

Like, . . .

Say . . .

Function: _____

Group D:

I'd like to say . . .

So, . . .

I'm going to talk about . . .

Function: _____

Group E:

In that case, . . .

Then, . . .

If that's true, . . .

Function: _____

👥 SPEAKING ACTIVITY 10

Choose one of the contexts below with your partner, then create and practise a dialogue of four or five lines using a variety of discourse markers.

1. You and your partner are discussing an event that you both witnessed.

2. You and your partner are discussing an event that only one of you saw.

3. You and your partner are comparing a gadget that you both own.

4. You and your partner are talking about a process that you both know.

👥 SPEAKING ACTIVITY 11

Yeah is the most commonly used discourse marker. Its most obvious use is to provide a direct affirmative answer, but actually its most common use is to acknowledge new information:

Example:

> Person A: That exam was tough.
>
> Person B: Yeah.

Yeah or *yes* can also re-acknowledge previously referenced information.

Example:

> Person A: I thought you said you'd already talked to the prof.
>
> Person B: Yes, you're right, I did talk to her.
>
> Person A: Yeah, yeah—I remember now—you went to her office yesterday.

Work with your partner to think of some other uses of *yeah*. You can use *yes* if you want to be more formal.

Communication Focus 3: Supporting a Proposition with Infographics

A proposition is a statement of a plan, offer, suggestion, or argument that you make to other people for them to consider and act upon. Examples and evidence that support a proposition are often best portrayed visually or graphically with an infographic or presentation software like PowerPoint.

When preparing your presentation documents:

- Label infographics and slides with clear titles.
- Avoid spelling or grammar mistakes.
- Minimize the amount of text in your infographic or on the screen and make sure the text is big enough for everyone to see.
- Source the information you are presenting.
- Follow a template colour scheme.
- If using presentation software, avoid animated text features.

When using presentation software or infographics:

- Avoid reading text off the screen—be prepared with a notecard.
- Do your best to maintain eye contact—spread it across the room like buttering bread.
- Point to your graphic using the closest hand, so that you are not reaching across your body.

SPEAKING ACTIVITY 12

A. Choose one of the following propositions to write about for sharing with a group of three of your classmates. You may need a few minutes and access to the Internet for fact-finding.

Propositions

- [City A] is a better place to live than [City B].
- The Internet strengthens democracy.
- English is an easy/difficult language to learn.
- I need my gadget.

B. Prepare a three-minute monologue with two main supporting ideas. You will need to support your chosen proposition with facts and examples. For each idea, develop a list of facts and examples.

Organize your monologue in this way:

- Introduction and statement of proposition
- Point 1 + support
- Point 2 + support
- Wrap-up + summary

C. When you are ready, share your monologue with your group. After everyone has had a turn, the group can discuss the effectiveness of clarity and support of points for each monologue presented.

SPEAKING ACTIVITY 13

Organize the information you gathered in the previous activity into an infographic. Revise the monologue from the previous activity in order to use your infographic as an effective support for your proposition. Prepare and practise your new presentation, and when you are ready, present your infographic and new monologue to the whole class.

PRONUNCIATION

Pronunciation Focus 1: Recognizing Thought Groups

Speakers use pauses to separate different key ideas. Punctuation is easy enough to see in writing, but good listeners recognize thought groups by finding the pauses speakers make to separate ideas.

PRONUNCIATION ACTIVITY 1

A. Listen to the sentences and identify the thought groups. When you are finished, compare your thought groups with your partner.

 **Track 38**

Example:

> **God / in his wisdom / made the fly / and then he forgot / to tell us why.** (Ogden Nash)

1. I've yet to meet anyone who can have only one pretzel and luckily there were lots made for the party.
2. The athletes have been missing curfew (in bed before 10:30) so management is considering measures to rectify the situation.
3. Once when I was four his glass eye fell out of its socket and rolled across the table finally wedging itself between the mashed potatoes and the salt shaker.
4. Tumon Bay is ideal for water sports but I prefer to relax indoors when I'm there.
5. The surf there runs a metre deep and 500 metres out and is the colour of a grasshopper cocktail.
6. The students kept speaking about food until their teacher agreed to let them have a break for lunch.

B. Listen again and repeat the sentences.

PRONUNCIATION ACTIVITY 2

A. Work with a partner to divide the following section of a political speech into what you anticipate the thought groups to be.

 **Track 39**

> To me / a good economy is one that makes sure / that every Canadian / has a real and fair chance at success. It means a thriving middle class one that provides growing incomes and job opportunities one that provides a real chance at joining the middle class for poorer Canadians. Productivity growth is important innovation is important. We want to make sure that the economy is diversified and resilient. But they are all means to an end. What we're after is an economy that provides well-paying good jobs for as many Canadians as possible. That's what fairness looks like.
>
> (Source: Excerpt from Justin Trudeau's major address to delegates at the 2014 Biennial Convention of the Liberal Party of Canada in Montreal on 22 February 2014.)

B. Now listen to Justin Trudeau's speech and adjust your answers as necessary.

Pronunciation Focus 2: Applying Thought Group Stress

 **Track 40** Multi-syllable words each have a stressed syllable. In English, each thought group will also have a primary stressed syllable that is louder, longer, or higher in pitch. Each thought group has its own rhythm because a speaker will apply **thought group stress** in order to communicate a certain focus to the listener. Good listeners can "catch" that focus by recognizing the change (in loudness, length, or pitch) within the thought group. Listen to the example sentences and notice which words are stressed.

Common thought group stress patterns:

Purposes	Examples
1. To give new information or clarify	I'm sorry; you are mistaken. I went to <u>Toronto</u> yesterday, not Montreal.
	You need to give a <u>persuasive</u> speech, not a narrative.
	You have to create an <u>account</u> for that.
2. To show emphasis or contrast	You think <u>you</u> are better?
	I have <u>never</u> said that.
	You thought I wasn't there, but I <u>was</u>.

 **PRONUNCIATION ACTIVITY 3**

Track 41 There are two important things to keep in mind when pronouncing thought groups.

1. Primary stress within thought groups is usually only placed on content words.
2. For any multi-syllabic word within the thought group, the stress remains in the same place as it would if the word were on its own.

The sentence "I dream of summer" has five syllables.

/ ai / drim / of / sum / mer / (five syllables)

Now listen to this sentence being pronounced five ways with a different syllable getting the primary stress each time. Pay attention to how the message changes slightly depending on which syllable is stressed.

Put a ✓ beside the stress patterns that sound natural and an ✗ beside the ones that don't sound natural, and explain why not.

1. / <u>AI</u>drimofsumer /　　＿＿＿＿
2. / ai<u>DRIM</u>ofsumer /　　＿＿＿＿
3. / aidrim<u>OF</u>sumer /　　＿＿＿＿
4. / aidrimof<u>SU</u>mer /　　＿＿＿＿
5. / aidrimofsu<u>MER</u> /　　＿＿＿＿

👥 **PRONUNCIATION ACTIVITY 4**

The sentence "These pretzels are making me thirsty" could have primary stress placed on a variety of syllables. Listen to each stress pattern and its meaning.

Stress Patterns	Meanings
These **pret**zels are making me thirsty.	It's the pretzels that are making me thirsty (not something else).
These pretzels are making me thirsty.	It is these particular pretzels that are making me thirsty (not any others).
These pretzels are making me **thirsty**.	I am surprised that the pretzels are making me thirsty.

In a thought group, primary stress cannot be placed on normally unstressed syllables. For example, *-els*, *-ing*, and *-ty* in the above sentences would never be stressed.

With a partner, take turns reading the five sentences in a smooth rhythmic voice, placing primary stress on different syllables in each thought group each time.

Remember! Place primary stress only on content words. Do not change the normal stress on multi-syllabic words.

1. I ate three cookies for breakfast.
2. I've never been to Canada's Wonderland.
3. It's getting colder outside.
4. My dad grows a moustache every year to collect money for Movember.
5. The Canadian Horseshoe Falls in Niagara are a spectacular sight to be seen.

👥 **PRONUNCIATION ACTIVITY 5**

A. You will hear some common English sayings. Listen to the example, and observe how the thought groups and primary syllable stress are marked. Then listen and mark thought groups and primary syllable stress on the other sayings.

 **Track 42**

Example:

/ Two wróngs / don't make a ríght /.

1. The pen is mightier than the sword.
2. When in Rome, do as the Romans do.
3. The squeaky wheel gets the grease.
4. When the going gets tough, the tough get going.
5. No man is an island.
6. Fortune favours the bold.

7. People who live in glass houses shouldn't throw stones.

8. A picture is worth a thousand words.

9. You can't make an omelette without breaking a few eggs.

10. Actions speak louder than words.

11. Practice makes perfect.

B. Practise saying the proverbs with a partner. When you are finished and confident about your pronunciation, choose one of the proverbs and present it to the whole class.

PRONUNCIATION ACTIVITY 6

Track 43

A. Work with a partner and listen to the stories. Draw a slash after each thought group and mark the primary stress (∕) for each one as you listen.

Story A:

Local sources report that Fred Barry of Algonquin Park has reported his 1997 Jeep missing after he had it painted with camouflage paint. Fred had been compelled to paint his Jeep after a recent incident in which his previous vehicle was stolen. He stated that at the time, he was looking for a feasible way to protect his property, but was upfront in admitting later that it may not have been a good idea. "It doesn't make sense to paint your vehicle with camouflage," stated police officer Gerardo Olivera. "You would need a tracking device to find your vehicle in the park!" Fred is posting information on social networking sites in an effort to seek help from the community. He claims to have received a few anonymous tips, but the location of his Jeep is still unknown. The Algonquin Police Service is hoping that this will be an isolated case, and that Fred's actions won't start a camouflaging initiative in the community.

Story B:

Catharine Barry was thrilled to find out that she had won $412,000 in the Lotto 6/49 draw last week. She stated that the win was a welcome distraction because her husband had lost his Jeep earlier this month after painting it with camouflage. Catharine decided to utilize the funds immediately. She worked out that she could take an elaborate four-week vacation to the Galapagos Islands with her family, buy her dream car, and purchase a beautiful cottage up north. When Catharine went to pick up her winnings so she could tap into her new wealth, she discovered that the amount was subject to the number of winning tickets. To her surprise, the winning number was linked to another ticket, which reduced her winnings by 50 percent, so she had to slightly alter her original plans. Catharine has been travelling around the world since receiving her newfound wealth but she still has her same old car, and the cottage up north remains a dream.

B. When you are finished, choose one of the stories and read it to your partner, focusing on accurate stress and rhythm.

PRONUNCIATION ACTIVITY 7

A. Listen to the dialogues and underline the focus you hear in each thought group.

 **Track 44**

Dialogue 1:

Person A: Are you going to the <u>lecture</u>?

Person B: Which lecture?

Person A: The environmental studies lecture. You know, it starts in five minutes.

Person B: Which room?

Person A: Oh, uhhm, I was hoping you were going to tell me.

Dialogue 2:

Person A: Are you watching this video on YouTube?

Person B: Which video?

Person A: The one where the cat is going crazy because the guy is using a laser pointer.

Person B: No, I'm watching a lecture on environmentalism. Try to focus on your studies, will you?

Person A: Oh, sorry, I was just taking a mental break.

Dialogue 3:

Person A: Your train leaves at seven.

Person B: The SkyTrain?

Person A: Yes, it leaves Waterfront at seven.

Person B: Waterfront or Burrard?

Person A: Waterfront, on the Canada Line.

Person B: What time's the next one?

Person A: Well, it leaves every six or seven minutes.

B. Practise the dialogues with your partner, applying effective stress as necessary. After you've practised, present one of the dialogues to the class.

PRONUNCIATION ACTIVITY 8

Practise reading the sentences below stressing the information the speaker wants to <u>emphasize</u>. Then, make your own original sentences.

1. I can bring my <u>book</u> to the test?
2. Amazon doesn't care whether you buy gadget <u>X</u> or gadget <u>Y</u>.
3. She told him to post it on <u>Facebook</u>, but he <u>tweeted</u> it instead.
4. I asked <u>you</u> to bring me a coffee, not her.

5. Tomorrow, the weather is supposed to be <u>nice</u>, at least that's what <u>I</u> heard.

6. _____

7. _____

PRONUNCIATION ACTIVITY 9

Track 45

The sentence "I went to class this morning." (/ aiwentuclasthismorning /) is one thought group with seven syllables but there would be only one primary stress, depending on what the speaker is focusing on or intending to get across.

A. Listen to each version of the sentence and note how stressing one syllable changes the message.

As you listen, pay close attention to how the stress pattern affects the meaning. Repeat each version, placing the stress on the same syllable as the speaker.

/ <u>AI</u>wentuclasthismorning / ➜ This would answer the question: "**Who** went to class this morning?"

/ ai<u>WEN</u>tuclasthismorning / ➜ This would answer the question: "**Didn't you go** to class this morning?"

/ aiwentu<u>CLAS</u>thismorning / ➜ This would answer the question: "**Where** did you go this morning?"

/ aiwentuclas<u>THIS</u>morning / ➜ This would answer the question: "On **which** morning did you go to class?"

/ aiwentuclasthis<u>MORNING</u> / ➜ This would answer the question: "**When** did you go to class?"

B. Practise saying the sentences aloud with a partner following the same rhythm and stress patterns as what you heard.

PRONUNCIATION ACTIVITY 10

With a partner, pronounce the following sentences, linking the words so each sentence becomes one multi-syllabic "word." Read each sentence aloud five times, shifting primary stress from first to second to third to fourth to fifth syllable each time. Alternate with your partner reading in a smooth, rhythmic voice.

1. I had a bad dream.
2. My soup's too cold now.
3. Your dog is too short.
4. That watch is so cheap.
5. This class is the best.

PRONUNCIATION ACTIVITY 11

Listen to the two example questions and answers, then practise asking each other the other questions and answering them, using the same stress and rhythm patterns as you've practised in the previous exercises. Remember to listen carefully to the stress and rhythm patterns and be careful to answer the questions according to your partner's intended meaning.

 **Track 46**

Example:

Question:	**What did you do yesterday?** (/ whatijiuduyesterdei / has seven syllables.)
Meaning 1:	Question: /whati**JIU**duyesterdei/
Response:	**Who, me? I went to Toronto.** → / hu**ME** / / **AI**wentutorono /
Meaning 2:	Question: /whatijiu**DU**yesterdei/
Response:	**Do? I went to a Blue Jays game.** → / **DU** / aiwentua**BLU**jaysgeim /

1. Where do you want to go?
2. What do you feel like having for dinner today?
3. Do you think it is going to rain?
4. Would you ever consider shaving your hair to support cancer research?

PRONUNCIATION ACTIVITY 12

Many changes have suddenly been made to the International Department workshops schedule below. Please update your partner by making announcements about the changes, stressing the information that has changed and needs to be <u>contrasted</u>. When you are finished, add two or three of your own changes.

Example:

Sorry everyone, the event is on June <u>18</u> (not June 15).

International Department Workshops, June ~~15~~ > 18		
~~08:00h~~ > 09:00h	Breakfast	Dining Room
10:00h	Group Organizing Strategies—~~Al Bond~~ > Tom Lucas	Rm 312
11:30h	Evaluation Strategies—Barbara Stansky	Rm ~~316~~ > 318
13:00h	~~Pasta~~ > Seafood Lunch	Main Hall
14:00h	~~Seminar~~ > *Pecha Kucha* sessions	Seminar Rm B
15:30h	Closing comments	Seminar Rm ~~A~~ > B
16:30h	~~Taxi~~ Airbus departure for airport	Lobby area

PRONUNCIATION ACTIVITY 13

Practise reading the following dialogue by placing thought group stress only on the speaker's <u>clarification</u>. Then, make your own original dialogue.

Person A: I'm in the Tourism and Hospitality program.

Person B: The two-year program?

Person A: No, the <u>four</u>-year program.

Person B: That's a diploma program, isn't it?

Person A: No, it's a four-year de<u>gree</u> program.

Person B: Sounds expensive.

COMMUNICATING IN THE REAL WORLD

Transcribing our own language provides insight into what we actually **do** say, not what we **think** we say or what we know we **should** say. This kind of reflection helps language learners improve oral accuracy. Carry out this transcription exercise by following the four steps below.

1. Organize a dinner party get-together with **two** of your friends. The three of you should use an audio-recording device—a cell phone would work—and record your **English** conversation over a period of approximately 15 minutes as you are discussing arrangements.

   Note:

   - This cannot be scripted; it must be natural speech.
   - Use language practised in this chapter (refer to Communication Focus 1 for inferences, and Communication Focus 2 for discourse markers).

2. Using your saved audio file, transcribe five minutes of any part of your conversation. Be detailed in your transcribing, recording as much as possible, including hesitations, repetition, and interruptions.

3. Print out and read your transcriptions. Reflect on your language as you read, asking yourself these questions:
   a. What were some of the assumptions and inferences we made?
   b. What discourse markers were used and how were they used?
   c. Did we overuse discourse markers (*uhhm*, *okay*, and *so*)?
   d. How did listeners ask for clarification or repetition?
   e. Are we satisfied with the level of vocabulary and pronunciation we used?
   f. What did we learn about our own language and conversation skills?
   g. What do we do well and what do we feel we need to improve about our language?

4. Make a brief written report of your reflections above and present it to the class orally using some of the skills from this lesson. Make an

infographic or table (showing, for example, the number and types of errors and discourse markers that were used) to support your presentation.

SELF-EVALUATION

Think about your work in this chapter. For each row in the chart sections **Grammar and Language Functions, Pronunciation, Learning Strategies**, and **Note-Taking**, give yourself a score based on the rating scale below and write a comment in the Notes section.

Show the chart to your teacher. Talk about what you need to do to make your English better.

Rating Scale

1	2	3	4	5

Needs improvement. ←————————————————→ *Great!*

	Score	Notes
Grammar and Language Functions		
making inferences		
using modals to express inferences		
using discourse markers		
supporting a proposition with infographics		
Pronunciation		
recognizing thought groups		
applying thought group stress		
Learning Strategies		
Speaking		
stating opinions		
Listening		
recognizing bias		
prioritizing ideas		
Note-Taking		
focusing on questions		
organizing with a visual system		

Vocabulary and Language Chunks

Look at this list of new vocabulary and language chunks you learned in this chapter. Give yourself a score based on the rating scale and write a comment.

revelations	adequate	caring capacity	it's all about . . .
legalistic	consent	blurring of boundaries	my gut tells me
jargon	reactive	the nature of	a thirst for
scam	sufficient	private sector	a conflict of interest
sham	underfunded	started out	the right call
surveillance	techblog	it tells us	all-consuming
ultimately	gear	business model	play mind games
anticipate	gadget	wade through the	
antiquated	novelty	sea of	
augment	materialism		
enticing	metrics		
up in arms	write-up		
legislation	trade show		
public sector	specs		
capacity	sameness		
infrared	affiliate		
infrastructure			

	Score	Notes
understanding new vocabulary and language chunks		
using new lexical items freely and confidently		

My plan for practising is _____

_____

_____

_____

CHAPTER 4

Our Relationship with Nature

THINKING AND TALKING

The relationship between humans and nature has grown increasingly problematic. In small groups, discuss the major effects people have on our environment and list them.

LISTENING 1

Before You Listen

👥 PRE-LISTENING ACTIVITY

Humans need clean drinking water to maintain their health. Pure water does not exist in nature—even nature's water contains a mix of chemicals and minerals. City officials and utilities managers around the country have the responsibility of maintaining secure, safe drinking water for the public.

In May 2000, in Walkerton, Ontario, seven people died from drinking local tap water poisoned by *E. coli* bacteria. In the same incident, 2,300 people became sick.

Read the article "Water in Canada by the numbers" and discuss the questions that follow with your partner.

Water in Canada by the *numbers*

1500: the number of water advisories (warnings of unsafe water) issued daily in Canada

12: the number of pharmaceuticals found in the St. Lawrence River

200: the number of pharmaceuticals and other human-made chemicals found in the Fraser River

80,000: the number of chemical products in use in North American homes and workplaces

548: the number of times per day someone in Canada visits the ER because of drinking water–related gastrointestinal distress *less than 50%:* the chance of having secure, safe tap water if you live on a First Nation reserve in Canada

almost 0: the number of male longnose dace (a fish) remaining in the Oldman River after sewage pollutants killed them off

90: the number of deaths per year in Canada credited to unsafe drinking water

(Source: Adapted from *Down the Drain: How We Are Failing to Protect Our Water*, by Chris Wood.)

Questions for discussion: When you are at home, do you drink the water from the kitchen tap, from a bottle, or from another source? How confident are you about the purity of the water you drink every day?

UPFRONT VOCABULARY

toxic cocktail	a poisonous mixture of different substances
take up	consume; absorb
Prozac	a drug used to treat the illness of depression*
estrogen	a hormone that promotes the development of female physical and sexual features
metabolism	the process of changing food into energy
effluent	liquid waste, especially chemicals from factories*

*Definition courtesy of *Oxford Advanced Learner's Dictionary.*

PRE-LISTENING VOCABULARY

A. Work with your partner to use context clues to complete each of the following sentences with a word from the box below. Use your dictionaries as necessary.

metabolism   pollute   hormone   pharmacist   depressed
diabetes   biologist   retrofit   municipal

1. A ____biologist____ studies living organisms in their environment.
2. Alice has _____, so she has to take medicine regularly to control her blood sugar level.
3. Sue Johnson became the mayor of our city by winning the last _____ election.
4. Kenji has a very strong _____; he can eat a lot food without gaining any weight.
5. I need to stop smoking in order not to _____ my body.
6. The mechanic was able to _____ Don's car so that it would accommodate his leg injury.
7. The local supermarket sells only _____-free meats.
8. My _____ often recommends no-name medicine.
9. It's better to take action to prevent pollution than just getting _____ about it.

B. Now work with your partner to discuss the meanings of the words in the part of speech (POS) table below, then practise making sentences with them. The italicized words are from the listening.

Noun	Noun (agent)	Verb	Adjective
metabolism	metabolizer	*metabolize*	*metabolic*
pollution	pollutant, polluter	pollute	*polluted*
hormones	n/a	n/a	hormonal
pharmacy	pharmacist	n/a	*pharmaceutical*
depressant	depressor	depress	depressed, depressing
diabetes	diabetic	n/a	diabetic
biology	biologist	n/a	biological
retrofit	retrofitter	*retrofit*	retrofitted
municipality	n/a	n/a	*municipal*

Note-Taking

 **Track 47**

Do you know what's in our drinking water? Chemicals from the pills we use in our daily lives are being mixed into it. In the CBC interview "Fish Swimming in Pharmaceutical Soup," Dr. Vance Trudeau talks about his research of the consequences when our waterways are polluted by a combination of drugs.

Listening STRATEGY

Listening for Cause and Effect

Recognizing the speaker's organization helps listeners understand. In addition to cause and effect (*if... then...*), other examples of organization include chronology (*first, next, finally*), and comparison (*whereas, moreover, on the other hand*).

First the interviewer explains the basic situation and then links the resulting effect to it:

> We take <u>billions of pills</u> a year and the <u>chemicals end up</u> in our rivers
> (key noun   +   *and* + key noun re-stated + new verb)
> and lakes.

Cause and effect can also be shown with expressions such as *with consequences for*, and *if ... then ...* :

> The chemicals end up in our rivers and lakes, with negative consequences for aquatic life.

> If sewage treatment plants are retrofitted, [then] they could remove small organic molecules.

Listen to the interview for the first time and complete the note outline by writing about the effects that chemicals have in each location.

Location of Chemicals	Effects of Chemicals
Waterways	

Location of Chemicals	Effects of Chemicals
Fish	
Drinking water	
Human body	

Listening for the Main Ideas

Listen to the interview "Fish Swimming in Pharmaceutical Soup" once again and add to your notes. Then use your notes to answer the questions. There may be more than one correct answer to each question. When you are finished, compare your answers with those of a classmate.

 **Track 48**

1. What is the cocktail effect a result of?

   ___ a combination of drugs

   ___ over-medication

   ___ a survey

2. What common pharmaceuticals does Dr. Trudeau say enter our waterways?

   ___ Prozac

   ___ contraceptives

   ___ aspirin

3. What are the main effects of an estrogen and Prozac mixture on male goldfish?

   ___ ovulation (egg production) can be stopped

   ___ egg yolk protein is produced and released into the blood

   ___ male reproduction is upset

4. What is the main recommendation Dr. Trudeau makes for other scientists?

   ___ to study the effects mixtures of chemicals have on humans

   ___ to observe the long-term consumption of these chemicals

   ___ to predict the effects of these chemicals on humans and fish

5. According to the listening, what does research confirm about how we consume these chemicals?

   ___ it's in our drinking water

   ___ it's in the fish we eat

   ___ it's in our sewage

6. What solutions does Dr. Trudeau recommend?

   ___ throw pills away when they have expired

   ___ retrofit sewage treatment plants

   ___ talk to local politicians

Listening Comprehension

 Track 49 Listen to the interview "Fish Swimming in Pharmaceutical Soup" once again and fill in the missing causes and effects, based on the information provided by Dr. Trudeau. When you are finished, compare your answers with those of a classmate.

Cause	Effect
We take billions of pills	the chemicals end up in our rivers and lakes
_____	the male goldfish liver produces egg yolk protein
_____	the male goldfish's reproductive ability is inhibited
a high level of estrogen in fish	_____
fish take up chemicals	_____
surveying other sewage technologies	_____
changing sewage plant procedures	
_____	they will talk to Members of Parliament

Personalizing

In groups, discuss the cleanliness of the waterways in towns and cities where you are from. Which picture more closely represents waterways from your hometown? Then, plan how you would begin and follow through on a campaign to protect local waterways as has been done for the river in the two pictures. Write down your ideas and share them with the class.

Vocabulary and Language Chunks

A. Work with a partner and match the language chunks with their usage.

Language Chunks	Meanings
1. make one's way into . . .	a. to express a cause and effect relationship
2. end up in . . .	b. to express the process of gaining a position
3. wherever there's . . . there's . . .	c. to express actual or practical experience
4. in the real world . . .	d. to express the total
5. when you add them all up . . .	e. to express a result

B. The common language chunks below are from the listening "Fish Swimming in Pharmaceutical Soup." Practise using the language chunks by building your own sentences with a partner.

make one's way into . . .

How big a problem is it that pharmaceuticals are *making their way into* the waterways?

_____

end up in . . .

And it *ends up in* the water, eventually.

_____

wherever there's . . . there's . . .

Wherever there's sewage, *there are* hundreds of chemicals.

_____

in the real world . . .

Actually, *in the real world*, there are hundreds or dozens of chemicals interacting.

_____

when you add them all up

And the effects that are being produced are clearly different, even *when you add them all up*.

_____

SPEAKING 1

Communication Focus 1:
Giving Instructions and Explaining Procedures

In the last two minutes of Dr. Trudeau's commentary, he suggested steps that begin the process of solving the problem of chemicals in our water. Notice how all Dr. Trudeau's instructions begin with a verb. This is a common way to give instructions.

> Research ozonation and reverse osmosis.
>
> Retrofit the sewage treatment plants.
>
> Find out what the best technology is.
>
> Talk to your municipal officials.
>
> Ask them what they are doing.

Grammar Note: Using the Imperative

Instructions, commands, rules, and procedures are expressed by a grammatical mood called the imperative. The imperative is formed by using the base verb without **to**. The subject is implied (not stated/written).

> **(You) Take photos only in the designated areas.**
>
> **(You) Recycle trash in the correct bins.**
>
> **(You) Return expired or unused pharmaceuticals to the pharmacist.**

The negative imperative is formed by **do** + **not** + base verb.

> **Do not leave your vehicle with its engine on while you are in the store.**
>
> **Do not flush expired or unused pharmaceuticals down the drain.**
>
> **Don't use your cell phone during class.**

Imperatives in request form use this: base verb + verb -**ing**.

> **Can you please refrain from feeding the animals in the zoo?**
>
> **Could you please avoid leaving garbage in the park?**
>
> **Would you mind turning off your cell phones?**

👥 SPEAKING ACTIVITY 1

Speaking STRATEGY 💬

Use sequencing words (transitions) to keep the flow of your instructions clear. Terms such as *first of all*, *secondly*, *then*, *before that*, and *after that* help explain a process.

As clearly as possible, explain to your partner step-by-step how to perform each of the tasks below. Briefly list the steps in the spaces below first. Remember to use transition words.

Example: Eat an orange.

1. First, peel the orange.
2. Then, separate the segments.
3. After that, remove the pith and eat.

Tasks:

Buy a cheap plane ticket.

Prepare drinking water.

Conserve water at home.

Grammar Note: Using Articles Correctly

The indefinite articles *a* and *an* are used to introduce nouns into a conversation or story for the first time to direct the listener or reader to the nouns.

The definite article *the* is used with nouns that have already been introduced—nouns which the listener or reader already has a context for.

Note:

1. Use *a*/*an* only for singular countable nouns:

   I sold him an old textbook.   How much is a cup of coffee?

2. Use *the* if . . .
   - it is likely that there is only one of the noun in the immediate building, town, or area:

   I'm going to the bank/library/post office/hospital/police station/beach.

   Where is the clock tower/main office/bookstore/washroom/clinic/registrar's office?

   Have you seen the sun/moon/prime minister/premier/mayor/king/queen?

   - there actually is only one (superlatives are formed on this principle of there only being one):

   the largest, the most expensive

3. Articles are usually not used with geographical names and other proper nouns:

   I have an appointment with Dr. Chikala.

   They spend summers in Banff, in Bow Valley near Bow River and Banff National Park.

   They have a cottage in Qualicum Beach, on Vancouver Island, near Horne Lake.

4. Remember: Sometimes *the* is built into the name of the place:

the St. Lawrence River, the Great Lakes, the Rocky Mountains, the Atlantic Ocean

SPEAKING ACTIVITY 2

Create a story chain. In groups of three, one group mate starts a story with the sentence "It was a sunny day" and adds one more sentence to follow it. Then in turn, each group member repeats all of the story prior to his or her turn, adding one more new sentence. Continue until everyone has contributed twice. Pay special attention to the use of indefinite articles each time objects are introduced to the story and definite articles when they reappear.

Example:

1. It was a sunny day. Ines saw a bird by a river.
2. It was a sunny day. Ines saw a bird by a river. The bird caught a fish in the river.
3. It was a sunny day. Ines . . .

SPEAKING ACTIVITY 3

Imagine that your partner will be travelling to your home country. Give your partner advice about being there. Give both positive and negative imperatives. After three or four minutes, switch roles.

Example:

In Guayaquil, Ecuador, don't flag taxis on the street. Instead, have the hotel concierge call one for you.

SPEAKING ACTIVITY 4

What would you say in the following scenarios? Work with a partner and use request form to express what you want the person to do.

1. Ask the person sitting in front of you in the movie theatre to stop talking.
2. Ask the person sitting beside you on the bus to give you some room.
3. Ask guests to take their shoes off when they come in.
4. Ask a classmate to repeat something the teacher said.

SPEAKING ACTIVITY 5

Work with a partner to list the steps required in the following procedures. Do your best to make your instructions clear using patterns from Communication Focus 1.

Example:

> to get accepted to a college or university in Ontario
>> Fill out the application on the website.
>>
>> Don't forget to include your high school transcript.
>>
>> Refrain from calling the colleges or universities before hearing back from them.

What are the steps?

- to pass the exam for this course

- to succeed at a job interview

- to establish a new law about water purity

SPEAKING ACTIVITY 6

With your partner, brainstorm examples from your own experience of different kinds of faulty instructions. Share your examples with the class.

Example:

> The assembly booklet that came with my new computer desk was too difficult.
>> too lengthy or too complicated
>>
>> unclear or ambiguous (two meanings) instructions
>>
>> illogical or incomplete sequencing of instructions
>>
>> a warning instruction given too late in a sequence

SPEAKING ACTIVITY 7

The following sentences are all ambiguous. Discuss the ambiguity of each with a partner and work together to improve the instructions.

- Bring your laptop to class if it looks nice tomorrow.
- Press ANY key to continue.
- Choose a partner with a book that is interesting.
- Keep your textbooks, and if your classmates are interested, sell them.

Communication Focus 2: Expressing Obligation

Depending on the situation, imperatives can be emphasized by changing loudness and tone of voice. For example, "GET OUT NOW!!" clearly shows strong and immediate obligation for someone to get out. It is highly important that the listener obey. Certain modal patterns can also express varying levels of obligation to the listener.

<u>You must</u> complete the assignment by Friday. (very strong obligation)

<u>You have to</u> complete the assignment by Friday. (very strong obligation)

<u>I urge you to</u> complete the assignment by Friday. (fairly strong obligation)

<u>It is required that</u> you create an account before you log in. (obligation)

<u>It is forbidden to</u> touch the turtles in this park. (obligation)

<u>It is advisable that</u> you filter the water before you drink it. (advisability)

👥 SPEAKING ACTIVITY 8

With your partner, choose which words should be emphasized in the following sentences. Then, practise saying them, emphasizing the key words and using a variety of tones of voice. Answers may vary from pair to pair.

1. Please leave the room immediately.
2. Do not ever say that to me again.
3. Could you try to eat a little bit more quietly, please?
4. To save money, buy home and auto insurance together.
5. If you really want to save water, take short showers whenever possible.
6. Would you mind doing your own work instead of using my ideas, please?

👥 SPEAKING ACTIVITY 9

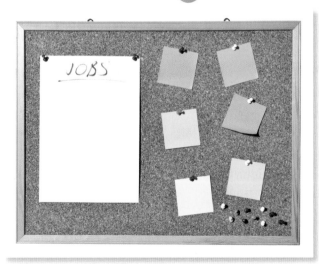

Working with your group, imagine that you are a management team at a place of business. Choose *one* of the following businesses and prepare a safety bulletin to inform your staff of their obligations (using *must, have to, must not,* and other modals).

a new hotel   a restaurant

a car rental company   a fitness club

other: _____

SPEAKING ACTIVITY 10

Take turns with your partner making requests using phrases such as:

Can you, *Could you*, and *Would you mind*

Example:

A door is locked.   →   Would you mind opening the door, please?

    →   Could you open the door, please?

1. You need someone to introduce a new person to you.
2. You need help with a translation.
3. You need to leave, but someone is in the way.
4. You need cash.
5. You don't understand a grammar point.
6. You don't know how to cook something.

SPEAKING ACTIVITY 11

With a partner, complete and practise the dialogue below using all the requests from Speaking Activity 10.

You: Hi, ___[partner's name]___, I'm sorry, but the door is locked, could you open it for me, please?

Partner: Sure, here you go. [opens door]

You: Thank you. Oh, there's someone there. Could you introduce . . .

SPEAKING ACTIVITY 12

Decide with your partner which of these items would be acceptable to bring to or wear in different situations, for example, a Blue Jays game, a movie, a job interview, or another situation of your choice. Use different levels of emphasis as you express obligations and advisability.

Example:

It is advisable that you wear a business suit to an interview.

It is inadvisable to wear a Leafs Jersey at a Senators game.

It is forbidden to bring your own lunch to a Blue Jays game.

| an apple | a box lunch | pepper spray | a business suit |
| a camera | a cell phone | a laptop | a Yankees cap |

LISTENING 2

Before You Listen

PRE-LISTENING ACTIVITY 1

Read the short article below and discuss the questions with a partner.

The "three Rs" have long been a part of Canadians' everyday vocabulary. It seems, however, that while Canadians understand the concept of "Reduce, Reuse, Recycle," they are not always so quick to comply. Recycling, if picked up at curbside, is easy enough for the common household to participate in. However, when it comes to separating recyclable plastic lids from compostable paper drinking cups, the three Rs are easily ignored. Notice that even when the appropriate bins are available side by side, empty cups with attached lids are often discarded into the waste bin.

What could be some of the reasons why people do this?

What can you do to raise awareness about the importance of the three Rs?

PRE-LISTENING ACTIVITY 2

Your teacher will give you a copy of The New Ecologist's infographic "Recycling by the Numbers". In small groups, discuss three of the most surprising statistics you can find here.

PRE-LISTENING ACTIVITY 3

Answer the questions for each of the following four topics:

recycling   global warming

banning the use of plastic bags   landfills

1. What do we already know about this topic? What do we still need to find out?
2. Why is this topic important to us? Why would we want to speak about it?
3. What are the causes? What are the effects?
4. What other topics are related to this one?

UPFRONT VOCABULARY

ballyhoo	unnecessary noise and excitement*
blight	sth that has a bad effect on the environment*

national average	a typical amount; the norm; common to the people of a country
bogus scheme	a plan, design, or program of action that is not genuine
city hall	the main building of the municipal government
methane (CH_4)	colourless, odourless gas that burns easily and comes from decomposing waste
diversion rate	a percentage of the total amount of waste that is reused and recycled

*Definition courtesy of *Oxford Advanced Learner's Dictionary.*

👥 PRE-LISTENING VOCABULARY

Work in small groups and try to think of as many synonyms for the following vocabulary as you can in 10 minutes. Then share your synonyms with the rest of the class; the group with the most synonyms wins.

Example: trash: garbage, waste, litter, junk, debris, refuse, effluent

recycled:
diversion:
diversion:
diversion:
skeptics:
boast:
falsify:
myths:
soiled:
potent:

After the groups have shared their synonyms, use a dictionary or thesaurus to find synonyms for the remaining words.

Note-Taking

It is everyone's responsibility to try to reduce or even eliminate the amount of waste we produce. We try our best to follow the three Rs: reduce, reuse, and recycle, and in this listening, you will hear about the efforts of the government and residents of one city to do more.

 **Track 50**

Think about how a report is organized to help you prepare and take notes. A well-organized report follows a standard IBC pattern (**I**ntroduction, **B**ody, **C**onclusion). Listen to the report "Can a City Produce Zero Waste?" paying attention to how this report is organized.

As you listen, add information from the report to the appropriate section in the basic outline.

Listening STRATEGY 🔊

Good listeners use their knowledge of transitional words and phrases (*let me begin . . .*; *first of all*; *secondly*; *finally*; etc.) to recognize these transitions as indicators of the IBC organization system.

Report: "Can a City Produce Zero Waste?"

Introduction (thesis statement, general background information about the topic):

Body (analysis and support of the thesis, main ideas, examples):

Conclusion (results, summary, optional final thought):

Listening for the Main Ideas

Track 51

While listening again to the report "Can a City Produce Zero Waste?" add further information to the notes you have already started, then use your notes to answer the main idea questions.

1. List four items from the report that can go into the compost bin.

   a.

   b.

   c.

   d.

2. How many residents have been fined by the city for incorrectly sorting their trash? _____

3. Other than its usual business of working with trash and recycling, what two things is Recology trying to do? _____

   _____

4. Quentin Kopp is a skeptic of San Francisco City Hall and Recology. What does he claim?

   _____

5. What is the difference between recycling and composting?

   _____

Listening Comprehension

Listen to the report "Can a City Produce Zero Waste?" once again and answer the comprehension questions. When you are finished, compare your answers with a partner and discuss any differences you may have.

 **Track 52**

1. When did San Francisco first require its residents and businesses to separate recycling, composting, and trash?

    a. 2009

    b. 2010

    c. 2012

    d. 2013

2. San Francisco currently has a ____ percent diversion rate compared to a national average of ____ percent.

    a. 35, 80

    b. 80, 100

    c. 100, 80

    d. 80, 35

3. How much could residents of San Francisco be fined for incorrectly sorting their trash?

    a. $10–200

    b. $300–500

    c. $100–1000

    d. $10–100

4. How big is Recology's compost facility in San Francisco?

    a. 100 acres

    b. 12 acres

    c. 23 acres

    d. 22 acres

5. How much food is converted to compost every day at Recology?

    a. 400 tons

    b. 200 tons

    c. 80 tons

    d. 40 tons

6. How much food waste goes directly to landfills in the rest of the country?

    a. 80 percent

    b. 100 percent

    c. 97 percent

    d. none of the above

7. According to Blumenfeld, how much of the food we buy at the supermarket ends up in the landfill?

    a. 97 percent

    b. 80 percent

    c. 50 percent

    d. 35 percent

8. Recology has created _____ jobs over the past _____ years.

    a. 180, 15

    b. 186, 10

    c. 100, 5

    d. 86, 10

9. San Franciscans pay about $_____ per month for their trash bins and $_____ for their recycling and compost bins.

    a. 28, 0

    b. 0, 28

    c. 28, 10

    d. 8, 0

Personalizing

Discuss the following questions with a partner.

1. Do you recycle? Why or why not?

2. What are greenhouse gases and why are they bad?

3. What could your school do to make recycling more attractive and easier for students?

Vocabulary and Language Chunks

Discuss the meaning of each language chunk from the report with a partner.

greenhouse gases	greenest city
(to be) in the middle of the pack	to face fines
to do audits	unbeknownst to them
to talk garbage	so far
to go along with sth	to have no doubt
to inflate figures	competitive bidding process

SPEAKING 2

Communication Focus 3: Managing a Discussion

Skilled speakers use certain words and phrases to navigate from topic to topic in conversations without disturbing the natural flow of language. Here are some phrases used in managing discussions:

> So, . . .
>
> Anyway, . . .
>
> As I was saying, . . .
>
> Where was I? Oh yes, . . . getting back to my (story, topic, initial idea), . . .
>
> Getting back to what I was saying, . . .

These expressions can also be combined:

> Anyway, as I was saying, there is a link between urban green space and health.
>
> So, getting back to my initial idea, the health impact of groundwater is significant.

👥 SPEAKING ACTIVITY 13

With a partner circle the examples of discussion management in the conversation below. Then, practise the dialogue together.

Sue: Hi, Bob, did you see the news today about that rainstorm in Halifax?

Bob: I sure did, Sue, it reminded me of a time when I was travelling in Turkey.

Sue: That's interesting, but as I was saying, in Halifax, many of the businesses near the waterfront were affected.

Bob: I know, I think it is going to cost the municipal government a lot of money to repair all the damages.

Sue: Anyway, you were saying it reminded you of your trip to Turkey. How so?

Bob: Right, where was I? Oh yes, when I was in Cappadocia, I stayed in a cave hotel, and can you believe it, they had Wi-Fi in the caves? It was brilliant!

Sue: Anyway, why did the rainstorm in Halifax remind you of Turkey?

Bob: Oh yes, getting back to my story. In Cappadocia, there was a similar rainstorm that washed away almost all the businesses in the area. Luckily, I had gone to Izmir just before that happened.

Sue: Wow, lucky you!

SPEAKING ACTIVITY 14

Based on what you learned in Listening 2, "Can a City Produce Zero Waste?", discuss these questions with a partner. Use discussion managing phrases from Communication Focus 3 to develop your ideas more completely.

1. Do you think it is possible for your family to produce zero waste? Why or why not?

2. What do you know about trash and recycling rules in your own city and country? Are there differences between there and where you live now in Canada?

3. Do you think cities should be able to impose laws and penalties on residents for not recycling?

SPEAKING ACTIVITY 15

Choose one of the five topics below. Begin a discussion with your partner on that topic. As you exchange ideas, use personal stories with examples and the expressions from Communication Focus 3 to maintain your discussion with your partner.

environmental pollution

waste processing in your hometown

recycling

littering

food packaging

SPEAKING ACTIVITY 16

Work in groups of three. Choose one of the topics from Speaking Activity 15 and begin a conversation. Each speaker should add his or her own ideas and example stories and occasionally let the conversation move away from the original topic. When you notice that the conversation has done that, try to change its direction and move it back to the original topic. Try to do this without stopping the conversation by using discussion management techniques.

Communication Focus 4: Developing a Proposal

Presenting a persuasive proposal is a communication skill that can be applied to many aspects of life. A proposal is a possible solution to an existing problem.

To develop a proposal:

1. Describe the problem.

2. Propose a solution with a clear outline that is supported with factual information.

3. List and discuss how the solution works.

4. Repeat steps 2 and 3 as necessary until the best solution is found.

Examples of phrases that can be used when weighing the pros and cons of a proposal:

> On the one hand/on the other hand . . .
>
> There are two sides to this argument . . .
>
> An argument for/against this would be . . .
>
> The advantages/benefits of . . . are . . .
>
> The weaknesses/disadvantages of . . . are . . .
>
> The result of . . . could be advantageous/beneficial/harmful
>
> There is a strong argument for the case that . . .
>
> There could be negative consequences to . . .

SPEAKING ACTIVITY 17

Work in groups of three and describe the problems that could be seen in each of the following. Start by stating what the problem is.

getting to school   school schedules   Canadian weather

Example: eating lunch

Problem: Students cannot find a suitable place to eat their lunch.
Description: The school cafeteria is a mess.
               The tables are covered in leftover food.
               Previous students have left their trash on the tables.
               There are spilled liquids on the floor.
               There are too many people.

SPEAKING ACTIVITY 18

Brainstorm with your group a list of the pros and cons of each of the following cases. When you are finished, share your lists with the class.

- travelling by car versus travelling by airplane
- doing pairwork versus working alone
- studying English in Canada versus studying it in your own country
- cohabiting before marriage versus waiting to get married before living together

Speaking STRATEGY

Identifying with your listeners by using their names during a discussion makes the conversation more personal, and therefore interesting, and retains the listeners' focus and attention.

Communication Focus 5: Making a Presentation

A presentation is a good way to communicate with an audience, whether it be a group of peers, a teacher, colleagues, or a manager. When preparing a presentation, there are five things to consider:

1. Objective: Why are you giving this presentation? What do you want your audience to gain?
2. Content: What are you going to talk about?
3. Organization: What is the outline of your presentation?
4. Audience: Who is going to listen? What are their needs?
5. Presentation: How will you use tone, body language, and software?

👥 SPEAKING ACTIVITY 19

With a partner, develop a proposal for each of the situations below. Provide a balanced perspective of the positive and negative aspects that you will use in presenting the case for your proposal.

- explaining to your parents that you would like to get a tattoo
- getting married to someone from a different nationality
- replacing your six-month-old smartphone with the newer version

👥 SPEAKING ACTIVITY 20

A common saying is "Necessity is the mother of invention": new inventions often come about because there is a need for a problem to be solved. Work with a partner to think of a product or idea that solves a problem. For example, bug spray is a product that solves a mosquito-bite problem; recycling is an idea that solves a waste problem.

Consider the five points in Communication Focus 5 and prepare a pair presentation for your class that includes a description of the problem and a proposal with an analysis. The class will vote which of the presentations is the most effective.

PRONUNCIATION

Pronunciation Focus:
Linking Words within Thought Groups

Avoid choppiness and talk with native speaker–like flow by linking words in thought groups together.

👤 PRONUNCIATION ACTIVITY 1

 Track 53

A. As you listen to the following sentences, note how the words in the thought groups are linked, and repeat each one.

- Type 1: Linking a consonant to the following vowel

   I eat a lot of vegetables.

   The prof handed out the tests.

   Look over the draft.

   I'm a little upset.

   Yours is the better idea.

   It was a degeneration of ideals.

- Type 2: Blending consonant to consonant (linking the same *continuant* sound)

  Drugs can alter reality.

  Students need to maintain a social life.

  Constrain neglect when possible.

- Type 3: Linking a vowel to the next vowel

  3 a. When the lips are **round** at the end of the first half of the link, it produces a **W** sound

  They go out every weekend.

  Who are the new students?

  The true answer is elusive.

---

  3 b. When the lips are **wide** at the end of the first half of the link, it produces a **Y** sound:

  I am graduating this term.

  He is making a generalization about the class.

  Please be aware of the fine print.

- Type 4: Assimilating (the first half of the link morphs into the second):

  He didn't like Pat's short paragraphs.

  Their perception of his shrewdness is wrong.

  The used textbook was a good buy.

B. With your partner, practise reading the sentences aloud, linking the words where indicated.

C. Create a sentence of your own for each type and write it in the space provided.

👥 PRONUNCIATION ACTIVITY 2

Fill in the blanks with words from the list below to complete the phrasal verbs. Then, practise saying the consonant-to-vowel-linked phrases with your partner.

hand   hold   put   give

depend   take   get

Example: (distribute) → <u>hand</u> out the papers.

Hint	**Phrasal verb**
(donate)	_____ away free goods
(submit)	_____ in the essay
(need)	_____ on my friends
(concede)	_____ in to an argument
(remove)	_____ off a wrapper
(dress)	_____ on a shirt
(exit)	_____ off a bus

👥 PRONUNCIATION ACTIVITY 3

Work with a partner to practise different types of linking. Create as many phrases as you can, using one item from each column. Write your phrases in the space provided. You may use any word more than once.

Example: see us off

see	us	the money	_____
be	all	you can	_____
show	it	again	_____
go	on	in	_____
try		off	_____
play		on	_____
			_____
			_____
			_____

👥 PRONUNCIATION ACTIVITY 4

Circle links in the news story on the next page, then take turns reading it with your partner.

Local News

A woman in Barrie, Ontario, is shaking her head after being robbed on Monday. Janice Applebee, 68, was walking her French poodle, Olivier, in Jessop Park. Mrs. Applebee had just finished scooping one of Olivier's messes into a plastic bag, when a young female dressed in jogging pants and a hoodie rushed by her, bumped her, grabbed the bag and sped off. Applebee is a little shaken, but says the robber can keep the plastic bag and its contents, a smelly present from Olivier.

PRONUNCIATION ACTIVITY 5

 **Track 54**

A. Listen to the following dialogue.

A: Hav-vyou god-da tic-ket?

B: Yes-sI do.

A: Gi-vit-to me please.

B: Here you-ware.

A: This haz-zex-pired.

B: Please lem-me-yin.

A: Can-nyu pay?

B: Not-today.

A: Sor-ry!

B. Now, practise the dialogue with your partner.

C. Together with your partner, read the next two dialogues and circle all the different types of links. Then practise speaking the dialogues.

Dialogue 1

A: Hey, you want to go to the movies with me?

B: Sure, that sounds awesome. What do you want to see?

A: How about that new movie with Emma Stone?

B: Oh yeah! I don't remember the name of it, but it looks really cool. She is a great actor.

Dialogue 2

A: Have you finished your assignment yet?

B: No, but I'm planning on doing that late tonight.

A: Are you sure? The teacher said we should stop procrastinating and get going right away.

B: I know, but I promised my parents I'd FaceTime during my break.

👥 **PRONUNCIATION ACTIVITY 6**

Take turns with your partner reading the phrases out loud and guessing what they really mean to say. When you have finished, make a dialogue using as many of the words as you can. Then present your dialogue to another pair.

Example:

Amos ooze → a masseuse

Ask rude arrive her   > _____

Ape arrow shoes   > _____

Isle of view   > _____

Pier steers   > _____

Sand tack laws   > _____

COMMUNICATING IN THE REAL WORLD

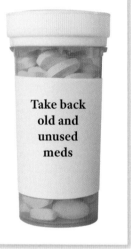

Take back
old and
unused
meds

Communities of neighbours around the world work together to clean up local rivers, sidewalks and streets, parks, and schools. In a competition with your classmates, work in small groups to create a proposal for an environmental clean-up activity. Each group should choose a different one. Within your group, follow the steps of Communication Focus 4 by describing the problem, proposing a solution, and explaining how the solution will work. Create a clear outline and make your proposal to the class, providing clear and concise instructions of what participants will need to do in order to take part in the activity.

After each group presents its proposals, the class will choose one for all to participate in.

SELF-EVALUATION

Think about your work in this chapter. For each row in the chart sections **Grammar and Language Functions**, **Pronunciation**, **Learning Strategies**, and **Note-Taking**, give yourself a score based on the rating scale below and write a comment in the Notes section.

Show the chart to your teacher. Talk about what you need to do to make your English better.

Rating Scale

| 1 | 2 | 3 | 4 | 5 |

Needs improvement. ⟵ ⟶ *Great!*

	Score	Notes
Grammar and Language Functions		
using the imperative		
giving instructions and explaining procedures		
using articles correctly		
expressing obligation		
managing a discussion		
developing a proposal		
making a presentation		
Pronunciation		
linking words within thought groups		
Learning Strategies		
Speaking		
using sequencing words		
identifying with listeners		
Listening		
listening for cause and effect		
recognizing transitions and sequencing		
Note-Taking		
organizing by cause and effect		
organizing by introduction, body, conclusion		

Vocabulary and Language Chunks

Look at this list of new vocabulary and language chunks you learned in this chapter. Give yourself a score based on the rating scale and write a comment.

toxic cocktail	national average	make one's way	(be) in the middle of
take up	bogus scheme	into. . .	the pack
Prozac	city hall	end up in	do audits
estrogen	methane	wherever there's . . .	talk garbage
metabolism	diversion rate	there's . . .	go along with sth
effluent	trash	in the real world	inflate figures
polluted	recycled	when you add them	greenest city
hormone	diversion	all up	face fines
pharmacist	compost	greenhouse gases	unbeknownst to them
depressed	skeptics		so far
diabetes	boast		have no doubt
biologist	falsify		competitive bidding
retrofit	myths		process
municipal	soiled		
pharmaceutical	potent		
depressant			
blight			

	Score	Notes
understanding new vocabulary and language chunks		
using new lexical items freely and confidently		

My plan for practising is _____

_____

_____

_____

The Influence of the Media

THINKING AND TALKING

How do people stay informed these days? Work in small groups to discuss how you personally access your news—local, national, and international. Do you interact with the news at all, and if so, how?

How is this different compared to the way previous generations accessed and responded to the news? Use the pictures to help guide your discussion.

LISTENING 1

Before You Listen

PRE-LISTENING ACTIVITY

Brainstorm with a partner and, in the space below, jot down what you think of when you hear the term *human rights*.

Then together, define the concept of *human rights* and write your definition on the lines below. Share your definition with the class and work together to add collocations for *human rights* to the mind map on the next page.

human rights: _____

_____

_____

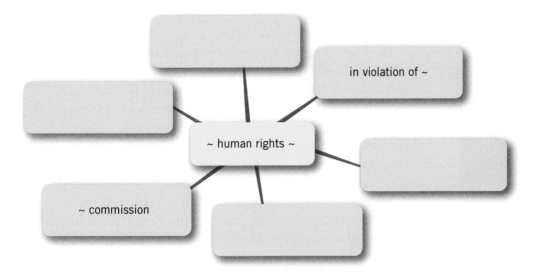

UPFRONT VOCABULARY

hurdle	a problem or difficulty that must be dealt with before you can achieve sth*
primary	main; most important*
media coverage	reporting of news through TV, radio, newspaper, Internet, etc.
corruption	dishonest or illegal behaviour of people in authority (political-, cultural-)*
state intervention	a government's involvement in a situation in order to improve it or help it
maladministration	the act of managing a business or organization in a bad or dishonest way*

*Definition courtesy of *Oxford Advanced Learner's Dictionary.*

PRE-LISTENING VOCABULARY

How well do you know each of the following words? Put a check mark in the appropriate column for each word. Then, find classmates who can help you understand vocabulary you are not certain about.

Vocabulary	I know and can explain.	I know but can't explain.	I am not certain.
(the) media			
element			
repercussions			
consequences			
poverty			
devastation			
(the) notion			
consequently			
bias			
to benefit others			

Note-Taking

 Track 55

What are our basic human rights? What interferes with people having access to these basic rights? You will listen to the round-table discussion "Hurdles to Ensuring Human Rights" with young human rights leaders participating in a global conference on human rights and diverse societies, being held at McGill University. You will hear the moderator of the round-table discussion manage the discussion by asking questions of the participants, who take turns in responding. In this discussion, you will hear the four participants answer questions regarding what they feel are the primary hurdles to protecting human rights and what solutions they would like to see implemented.

Listen to the round-table discussion for the first time and add information from each speaker to the mind map.

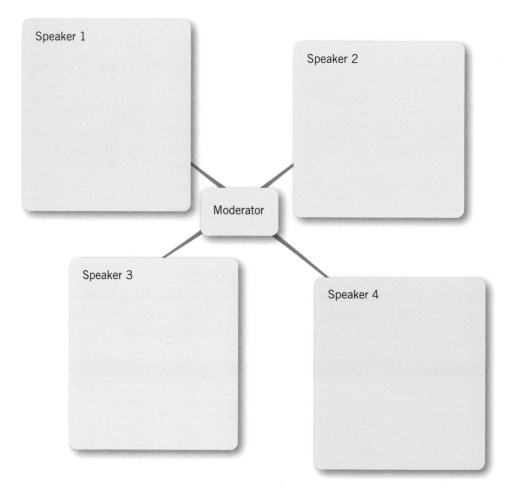

Listening STRATEGY

Visualizing the mind map allows you to easily observe how points and ideas are added by each speaker as you listen. This mental organization of the round-table discussion is also enhanced by following how the moderator clarifies questions and answers and redirects the discussion.

Listening for the Main Ideas

 **Track 56**

Listen to the round-table discussion again and use your mind map to answer the questions below. When you are finished, compare your answers with those of a classmate.

1. The moderator asks two main questions regarding human rights. What are they?

    a. _____

    b. _____

2. According to the speakers, what is the primary hurdle to protecting human rights?

    _____

3. What is another hurdle to ensuring human rights?

    _____

Listening Comprehension

Listen to the round-table discussion again and answer the six questions. When you are finished, compare your answers with those of a classmate.

 **Track 57**

1. Which of the following does the first speaker **not** indicate as an issue with the media?
    a. The media are often difficult for the general population to access.
    b. The media bring issues to the attention of people around the world.
    c. The media are not responsible enough in gaining understanding of local issues.

2. What are some of the difficulties the second speaker does **not** explain regarding people's access to the media in Afghanistan?
    a. lack of electricity due to poverty
    b. deficiency of education resulting in people's inability to digest content
    c. disinterest by people in general

3. According to the third speaker, the media are responsible for:
    a. informing public opinion
    b. influencing public action
    c. both a and b

4. The third speaker suggests that the media should:
    a. provide multiple sources of unbiased information
    b. offer a variety of biased sources
    c. influence the population to enforce human rights

5. What hurdle does the fourth speaker describe regarding human rights in Greece?
    a. devastation
    b. corruption
    c. deprivation

6. What do the media do well according to all speakers?
   a. they bring a variety of issues to the attention of the public
   b. they prompt the public to action or inaction
   c. both a and b

Personalizing

The same way that media have a social responsibility to provide information to the public, businesses should have a socially responsible business model in order to reduce international human rights violations. In small groups, make a list of three businesses that practise social responsibility and describe how you feel they do this. When you are finished with your lists, share them with the class.

Vocabulary and Language Chunks

Work in groups of four and match the language chunks with the appropriate synonyms. When you are finished, take turns acting out one random language chunk at a time, and have your group guess the language chunk you are trying to convey. Use exaggerated movement and no speaking in your pantomime.

Language Chunks	Synonyms
1. point (sth) out	____ regardless
2. take note of sth	____ make s/o aware of sth
3. to better sth (v.)	____ best
4. carry on (and on)	____ continue
5. have access to sth	____ shortage
6. lack of sth	____ improve
7. play an important role	____ emphasize
8. no matter what (s/o says)	____ be allowed entrance
9. bring sth to s/o's attention	____ notice
10. the ultimate (person, thing)	____ perform a vital task

SPEAKING 1

Communication Focus 1: Beginning a Group Presentation

There are a number of considerations involved in getting a panel discussion, seminar, or team presentation off to a good start. A host needs to set the tone, introduce the topic, and put the presenters in the context of the event.

- Introducing the speakers to an audience is the first step. It is an opportunity to establish the credibility and expertise of the speakers and their team.

  I'd like to introduce Joachim Ladner, an expert in traffic safety issues . . .

  To my right is Maria Oliveros, a post-doctoral scholar in civil law at UBC . . .

  It is my pleasure to introduce Dan Potashner, who has 30 years' experience in the field of civil rights . . .

- In a panel discussion or debate, where the speakers may not share the same thesis or opinions, it is helpful to clarify speakers' positions or backgrounds for the audience.

  Representing the argument for bicycle helmet laws, we have Chuntao Luo, from CCB Helmet Co.

  Speaking against bicycle helmet laws is Ahmad Al Thobiati, from the regional police department.

- The interaction among members of a team presentation also contributes to setting the tone of a presentation or formal discussion. The team's body language (eye contact, gestures, facial expression, positioning) can indicate interest in the topic and support of the opinions being expressed. Successful teams often thank each other and refer to each other by name.

- Vocabulary choices complement the tone. Words and phrases used may be, for example, professional, academic, or casual and may be used to set or match the desired tone. Consider these two ways to express essentially the same thing:

  You guys probably all think that bike helmets are good, but we don't think that that is important when we're talking about laws that force us to wear them.

  Although we may agree with the audience that a bicycle helmet is an effective safety device, this point is not relevant to our discussion about the necessity of laws that make its usage mandatory.

- Remember! Stating a topic is not the same as making a thesis statement. Stating the topic lets the audience know what you are going to talk about while making a thesis statement explains your position on this topic.

We are here to talk about bicycle helmet laws. We feel that they are an unwanted, unnecessary infringement on personal rights and freedoms.

- A rhetorical question, a quote, a "shocking" statement, a photo, or a short video can be an effective way to immediately gain the audience's attention, and help them think about the topic.

Is wearing a bicycle helmet safer than not wearing one? Of course it is.

Jean-Jacques Rousseau said that "Man is born free, and everywhere he is in chains."

- Knowing the needs and interests of the audience helps keep them focused.

Approved bicycle helmets can cost from $50 to $250 per helmet per child per growth stage, and bicycle helmets are often lost or stolen. Most family budgets in this town cannot afford $1,000 for bicycle helmets.

- Making a local reference can show that the speaker is interested in the audience and speaking for their benefit.

In this town, you have a 31-year-old bylaw that requires adults to wear bicycle helmets. At the same time, the town only has four police officers on street patrol at any given time. Can you imagine your police force chasing people up and down Canal Street trying to catch up to and ticket cyclists?

- An icebreaker (an activity that sets a relaxed mood) can help participants feel comfortable. Sometimes an icebreaker will involve humour.

I was watching a cyclist approaching and couldn't tell if he was riding a touring bike or a mountain bike—and then, it hit me!

What's the hardest part about riding a bicycle? Answer: The pavement.

SPEAKING ACTIVITY 1

Working in groups of three, ask each other questions to try to find out what the group members' particular life highlights are. Then, use language from the Communication Focus and what you have learned about each other to introduce the person on your right to the person on your left. Continue until all three of you have had a chance to introduce someone.

Areas that you might highlight in an introduction include:

- experiences: work, research, travel, events
- skills: organizational, research, leadership, communication
- education: accomplishments, awards

Speaking STRATEGY

Introducing people to each other is a great way to build social networks. At this time, people often exchange business cards or social networking information.

SPEAKING ACTIVITY 2

Work with a partner and tell each other the qualifications you currently have that would assist you in getting work. List each other's relevant background and qualifications on a piece of paper, then get together with another pair. You will each take turns introducing your partner. Give at least three sentences that describe your partner's expertise.

Example:

Ali: Hello, I would like to introduce you to Bob. He's a student in the Hospitality Management program. Bob is in his last term of study, and he's been working at the front desk of the DoubleTree for two months.

Cory and Dani: It's nice to meet you, Bob.

Cory: Thank you for introducing Bob to us, Ali. It's a pleasure to meet you, Bob. Can you tell me more about your experience working at the DoubleTree? I was considering applying there for a summer job.

Bob: Sure, but first, I'd like to meet your friend.

Cory: Certainly, let me introduce Dani. . .

The discussion continues until everyone has been introduced.

SPEAKING ACTIVITY 3

Work in small groups and brainstorm qualifications you would need to have in order to do well in the professions listed below. Then take turns introducing each of the professionals and their qualifications to the group.

Example:

Teacher needs teaching degree, fluency in language of instruction, provincial teaching licence

Susan (to potential employer): Ms. Anderson, I'd like to introduce you to Andrea. She has recently graduated from Brock University with a bachelor's degree in education. She speaks English as well as French with native-like proficiency, and is licensed to teach children in Ontario.

Professions:

winemaker	hotel manager	chef	mechanic	hairstylist
engineer	lawyer	doctor	linguist	

SPEAKING ACTIVITY 4

Work with your partner to list what you think the audience needs are in the context of the following presentations.

Examples:

Topic: plagiarism   Audience: post-secondary students

Needs: to know what plagiarism is, what the consequences of plagiarizing are, how to cite sources

Topic: **student on-campus dining satisfaction**   Audience: **cafeteria management**

Needs: **to know what students think about the present dining choices available; what students like and dislike; what other food options are available; what the costs and feasibility of other options are**

Topic: job fair   Audience: post-secondary students

Needs:

Topic: homework   Audience: post-secondary teachers

Needs:

👤👤👤 SPEAKING ACTIVITY 5

Working in groups of three, list and discuss strategies you would use to gain the audience's attention in the following scenarios or one of your own. Your attention "grabber" could be an activity or a statement.

Examples:

Scenario/Topic: **You are beginning a presentation about issues involving smartphone usage.**

Thesis: **Although there are advantages to using a smartphone, their use in academic settings has created many problems.**

"Grabber" (statement/question):

1. **"How many times have you been annoyed by a smartphone buzz, or worse, the loud voice of someone talking on a phone?"**

OR

2. **"Smartphone distraction has been linked to falling grades, failure, and expulsion."**

"Grabber" (activity):

1. **Show a video or PowerPoint on the screen, and arrange for a smartphone to buzz while you're talking.**

OR

2. **Do a poll of all the participants in the room, for example, asking how many use smartphones in class, at work, while driving, etc.**

Scenario/Topic: You are beginning a presentation about first language usage in the ESL classroom

Thesis:

"Grabber" (statement/question):

"Grabber" (activity):

Scenario/Topic:

Thesis:

"Grabber" (statement/question):

"Grabber" (activity):

Communication Focus 2: Participating in a Panel Discussion

Speakers on a panel are selected because they bring their expertise and perspective to a discussion. When speakers discuss ideas, they use varying degrees of certainty to emphasize their points.

> ### *Grammar Note:* Expressing Degrees of Certainty

Certainty can be expressed in both the positive as well as the negative sense.

> I am certain that fruit is delicious when it is ripe. (I am certain of the positive)

> I am certain that fruit is **not** delicious before it is ripe. (I am certain of the negative)

The word *uncertain* is neither positive nor negative.

> I am **uncertain** whether a fruit is ripe.

Using adverbs of certainty adds complexity and precision to language by specifying exactly the degree of certainty of the speaker.

Degree of Certainty	Adverbs of Certainty
high level of certainty	definitely
↑	certainly
	likely
↓	probably
low level of certainty	possibly

> That is <u>definitely</u> the best apple.
> That is <u>certainly</u> the best apple.
> That is <u>likely</u> the best apple.
> That is <u>probably</u> the best apple.
> That is <u>possibly</u> the best apple.

To show a negative sense of certainty, add the word ***not*** following the adverb.

> That is <u>probably not</u> the best apple.

Note: The sentence "It is (not) likely" can be used in conversation as a stand-alone expression when commenting on something.

👥 SPEAKING ACTIVITY 6

With a partner, take turns to finish the sentences stating different degrees of certainty for the situation below.

Situation: leaving my house

Positive	**Negative**
I will <u>possibly</u> leave my house today.	I will <u>possibly</u> *not* leave my house after today.
I will <u>probably</u> leave my house <u>before 8:00 am</u>.	I will _____.
I will <u>likely</u> leave my house _____.	_____.
I will <u>certainly</u> _____.	_____.
I will <u>definitely</u> _____.	_____.

👥 SPEAKING ACTIVITY 7

Work in small groups and discuss each of the following topics stating your opinions with varying degrees of certainty.

consequences of poverty　　free speech　　repercussions of the Internet

Example:

I am certain that poverty negatively affects personal health.

👥 SPEAKING ACTIVITY 8

For one of the situations below, create a short dialogue with a partner. In your dialogue, refer to the grammar note and include some statements reflecting various degrees of certainty. Practise speaking the dialogue and when you feel ready, present it to the class.

take a vacation　　finish homework　　attend college　　buy fair-trade coffee

👥 SPEAKING ACTIVITY 9

Work together in small groups and talk about the importance of learning English for you personally. Each speaker should apply personal knowledge of how English is taught and its relevance in his or her own country and its educational system.

LISTENING 2

Before You Listen

👥 PRE-LISTENING ACTIVITY 1

Work with a partner and use the story below as the content for a race against other pairs. The first pair to accurately answer the question correctly wins the competition.

Instructions:

Student A: Read the first half of the story to yourself. Close your book and report what you can remember of the story to your partner (B). If you forget, go back to the story as needed.

Student B: Close your textbook and record on paper the story your partner tells you.

At the midpoint of the story, change roles.

The Story:

[Student A reads] A father and his son are playing soccer together when the two of them trip over each other and are seriously injured. The father has a dislocated disc in his back, and the son, a broken ankle. They are both taken to the nearest hospital.

[switch]

[Student B reads]: The father and his son are immediately attended to by two different physicians in two separate operating rooms. The father's surgery is immediately under way; however, the son's doctor looks surprised and exclaims: "I can't operate on him! This is my son!"

How can this be?

👥 PRE-LISTENING ACTIVITY 2

With a classmate, make a list of three Canadian businesses that you know. They can be small local businesses like restaurants or shops or large corporations. Next, do a web search to find out the owners, managers, or CEOs in these companies. Consider your results in discussing the following questions.

1. Are both genders equally represented in the senior management positions?

2. Do you think this is the same as or different from businesses in your country?

3. Now think about some international corporations or governments. Is there a gender balance in top positions?

UPFRONT VOCABULARY

editor-in-chief (EIC)	person who is in charge of a newspaper, magazine, etc.
day one-er	person who has been with a company since the very beginning
male-dominated	more men than women
pushy	trying very hard to get what you want, especially in a way that seems rude*
bossy	always telling people what to do*
code	a system of words that represent a secret message
columnist	a journalist who writes articles for a newspaper or magazine

*Definition courtesy of *Oxford Advanced Learner's Dictionary.*

PRE-LISTENING VOCABULARY

Work with a partner to match the following words with their synonyms.

1. distinguished   ____ disadvantage, drawback, flaw
2. scrutiny   ____ analysis, inspection, surveillance
3. gender   ____ sex, feminine, masculine
4. uncertainty   _1_ acclaimed, brilliant, dignified
5. downside   ____ ambiguity, confusion, skepticism

When you are finished matching, complete these sentences with synonyms of the vocabulary in parentheses.

1. Good language learners are comfortable with _____ (ambiguity) and are willing to make language mistakes they can learn from.

2. There is no _____ (drawback) to eating healthy food.

3. The security guard looked at her driver's licence with _____ (close inspection) to make certain she was old enough to enter the club.

4. She has had a long and _____ (dignified) career; she has worked for many famous and respected companies.

5. Even in the 21st century, _____ (sex) inequalities exist in the workplace.

Note-Taking

What types of jobs are more likely performed by women? What positions do men more commonly hold? Do you believe that both men and women are equally qualified for all types of work? You will listen to an interview with former CBC host Jian Ghomeshi and his guest Anne Marie Owens, who is about to begin in her new position at an important Canadian newspaper. They discuss gender equality in the workplace.

Prepare a notes chart to use during the listening by dividing a sheet of paper into two sections, questions and answers. Be sure to allow more space for the main points of the answers, as this is where you will gain the most content from an interview.

Questions (Ghomeshi) | **Answers** (Owens)

Listening STRATEGY

A one-on-one interview usually follows a standard question and answer format. Good listeners anticipate (predict) possible answers and follow-up questions before they hear them.

Listening for the Main Ideas

A. As you listen to the interview for the first time, write Ghomeshi's questions in the left-hand column of your notes chart. When you have finished listening, compare your notes with a partner to confirm you heard Ghomeshi's questions correctly.

 **Track 58**

B. With your partner, discuss the questions below and answer them together.

1. What, according to Ghomeshi, seems a little ridiculous?
2. Does Owens consider the media industry to be male dominated?
3. Does Owens feel that she has personally been treated differently than men in similar positions? Explain.
4. How does taking this new role during tough and uncertain times weigh on Owens's mind?

Listening Comprehension

Listen to the interview again, and add Owens's corresponding answers to the notes you started in the previous activity. Discuss and compare your notes in small groups, then answer the questions using your notes.

Track 59

1. What is Anne Marie Owens's new job?
2. What is the name of the company Owens will work for?
3. How does Owens feel about her new job?
4. What is "the woman thing"?
5. How long has Owens been "in the industry"?
6. How does Owens feel about "the business" with regard to gender equality?
7. Why does Owens want the job?
8. What does Owens like most about the company she will work for?
9. What is the start date of Owens's new job?
10. In Owens's opinion, why were the two female national Canadian newspaper editors fired?

Personalizing

Work with a partner. Choose one of the following:

A. Put yourselves into Ghomeshi's and Owens's shoes. Think about what other questions you would ask Owens. How do you think Owens would respond? Practise this hypothetical interview, and then perform your role-play in front of the class.

B. Pretend that you are interviewing one of the following famous people. What would you ask them regarding gender equality, the importance of the media, or social responsibility? How do you think they might answer? Practise this hypothetical interview together, and then perform your role-play in front of the class.

Donald Trump

Oprah Winfrey

Albert Einstein

Benazir Bhutto

Vocabulary and Language Chunks

Use the context in the following sentences to help you understand the meaning of the underlined language chunks that were used in the interview. Write your definition of the language chunk in the space, and when you are finished, compare answers with your classmates.

1. If the team wins again tomorrow night, they will <u>make history</u>.
   to make history = _____

2. She's been <u>rising through the ranks</u> very quickly ever since she started working here.
   rising through the ranks = _____

3. One day, I'd like to have the <u>top job</u> at this place.
   top job = _____

4. Volunteering was <u>a move in the right direction</u> for me; I certainly will get a better job because of it.
   a move in the right direction = _____

5. My wife <u>took me by surprise</u> when she booked an Arizona road trip for just the two of us.
   take s/o by surprise = _____

6. The fact that he was a terrible nurse <u>was ascribed to</u> his gender, when his lack of motivation was in fact the real cause.
    to be ascribed to = _____

7. We are living in a <u>time of flux</u> due to more and more readily available information on the Internet.
    a time of flux = _____

8. "<u>Right on</u>, I completely agree!" he shouted, enthusiastically.
    right on = _____

9. I think I may have made a mistake, and it's been <u>weighing on my mind</u> for some time now.
    sth weighs on one's mind = _____

10. He hasn't been working very hard and knows it's time to <u>pull himself up by his bootstraps</u>, or he'll likely get fired.
    to pull oneself up by the bootstraps = _____

11. He decided to <u>take a gamble</u> and ask his classmate if she wanted to go to dinner with him.
    to take a gamble = _____

12. They were such a <u>ragtag</u> group of people from entirely different backgrounds and with different visions of the future.
    ragtag = _____

SPEAKING 2

Communication Focus 3: Moderating a Panel Discussion

Panel discussion is an academic presentation style of exploring a variety of perspectives about important ideas and issues. It's a type of formalized conversation. Panels are used in order to draw attention to issues, or raise awareness about them.

In order to manage a panel discussion well, moderators must ensure that all speakers get an equal opportunity to speak, discuss each other's perspectives, and respond to each other's points.

There are some guidelines a moderator must follow:

Speaking STRATEGY

Moderators draw attention to the main points, illustrating them to the participants, but they must be careful to meanwhile maintain a neutral position.

Do	Don't
introduce the idea/issue	introduce your own bias
introduce the panellists	include irrelevant information
use panellists' names when addressing them	assume audience knows
have general knowledge of the subject	act as one of the experts
manage time; interrupt when necessary	let any speakers dominate
thank panellists and audience	

Grammar Note: Using the Subjunctive Mood

The subjunctive mood can express purpose and intention, and can be used in the past or present.

The main verb remains the same as the present form (except in the third person where the -*s* is dropped). To negate a subjunctive form, simply add **not** before the verb.

Positive	Negative
I **suggest that** she **pay** the bill.	I suggest that she **not pay** the bill.
Yesterday I **suggested that** she **pay** the bill.	Yesterday I suggested that she **not pay** the bill.

In the subjunctive mood, the verb *be* remains in its infinitive form, except in conditional sentences where we use the past form *were*.

> I demand that they *be* here.

> I insisted that she *be* present.

Conditional: **If she *were* more punctual, she would have caught the bus.**

The subjunctive is often preceded by verbs like *insist*, *demand*, *recommend*, *suggest*, *order*, *prefer*, and *request*. The verbs can also be preceded by certain adverbs like *strongly*, *kindly*, *cordially*, or *sincerely*.

These adverbs are used to give more information about the intent, intensity, or tone of the verb.

Positive	Negative
Present	
I kindly insist that I pay for your dinner.	I insist that I not pay for your dinner.
He demanded that he remain anonymous.	He demanded that he not remain anonymous.
It is recommended that you lock your doors.	It is recommended that you not lock your doors.
We strongly suggest that you leave now.	We strongly suggest that you not leave now.
Past	
We highly recommended that they attend.	We highly recommended that they not attend.
The audience requested that she speak louder.	The audience requested that she not speak louder.
Past (conditional)	
If he were here, we'd be finished by now.	If he were not here, we'd be finished by now.
If there were more people using Twitter, news could spread faster.	If there were not more people using Twitter, news could spread faster.

👥 SPEAKING ACTIVITY 10

Below is a list of common verbs that can be used in the subjunctive. Take turns making a statement about each situation listed, using the verb beside it in the subjunctive. Follow the examples in the Grammar Note to help you construct your sentences.

Example: We ask that you not speak your first language during class.

Verbs	Situations	Statement
ask	speak first language during class	
advise	study for a test	
demand	return a borrowed book	
insist	buy a coffee	
prefer	go shopping	
suggest	find a quiet place to study	
propose	go to a restaurant	
recommend	stay in a hotel	
request	attend an event	
urge	practise	

Note that the verbs *hope*, *expect*, and *want* are **not** commonly used in the subjunctive.

👥 SPEAKING ACTIVITY 11

Practise directing a conversation by inserting commentary and asking other participants to provide their perspectives. In groups of four, select one of the topics below and discuss it in as much depth as you can. One person will speak at a time and the listeners should take turns moderating the discussion, that is, thanking the speaker and asking another group member to add his or her perspective.

Topics:

social responsibility   food   sports   education

environment   other: _____

Example:

Alison: It is likely that tofu will replace all meat consumption in the near future.

Bob: Thank you for your opinion. Carlo, do you have something to add to this idea?

Carlo: Yes, I definitely agree with Alison, and I would like to add

_____.

Donna: Carlo, thank you for your point of view. Bob, do you agree with Alison as well?

Bob: . . .

SPEAKING ACTIVITY 12

Sometimes a discussion will go off topic, or one speaker will take over too much of the conversation. Here's an activity to practise refocusing and redirecting those discussions and speakers.

In groups of three, start a conversation about one of the topics in the list below. One speaker will try to change the topic to another one in the list. When the discussion changes, another speaker will redirect by asking questions and getting the conversation back to the main discussion. The discussion is finished when all participants have had a chance to do each of these at least once: speak, change the topic, and redirect.

Topics:

homework assignment   group assignment   job interview

dinner plans   organizing a party   grocery shopping

SPEAKING ACTIVITY 13

Work in groups of three and brainstorm supporting ideas for two different points of view about one of the following topics. Then choose a role for each of your group members (moderator, first panellist, second panellist) and practise a panel discussion. When you are ready, present your panel discussion to the class.

Example:

Topic: **human rights regarding child labour**

Point of View A: **Children should never have to work, ever.**

Support (of POV-A):

- If children are allowed to work there will be abuse: employers and even parents will abuse the system.
- Children do not have the maturity to make work-related decisions.
- Children's bodies are not completely formed, so making them work could have negative long-term physical effects.

Point of View B: **There are times when children can and should have jobs.**

Support (of POV-B):

- Many successful businesspeople delivered newspapers or helped family businesses in their youth. Nobody is hurt by that, and children learn entrepreneurship that way.
- If children want to work, and their parents are willing, it's a free country.
- Some families need the income relief that working children can provide.

Topics:

| human rights | activism | awareness raising | volunteering |
| the media | fair trade | animal rights | women's rights |

Communication Focus 4: Explaining Complex Ideas

Most people understand and learn best when they are interested in a topic and they can understand the language that is used in the explanation. When explaining complex ideas to someone, it is helpful to make a connection between the listener's current understanding of the world and then expand on that understanding. To help listeners grasp concepts more easily, speakers commonly use analogy (an association of a complex idea to a more familiar one) and anecdote (a short, personal story).

A description of the Swiss Canton system using a Canadian analogy:

> Switzerland has 26 cantons. Someone living outside of Switzerland may not understand the word *cantons*. To explain this complex idea, we may use the analogy that "Cantons are like small Canadian provinces" because this is a concept readily understood by Canadian listeners.

An anecdote illustrating making mistakes while learning a language:

> Tom, an ESL student, was looking for his friend Catherine because he had to return something he had borrowed from her. He decided to ask someone that he knew was an acquaintance of Catherine. Here is the discussion they had:
>
> Tom: Excuse me; do you know who my friend Catherine is?
>
> Eden: Yes, of course.
>
> Tom: Well then, who is she?
>
> Eden: Well, she's your friend; certainly you know who Catherine is.
>
> Tom: I really need to know who she is. I must return something to her!
>
> Eden: Oh! You mean <u>where</u> she is? She left a few minutes ago to catch her bus; if you go quickly, you might still find her.
>
> Tom: Thank you, yes, *where* is what I meant.

👥 SPEAKING ACTIVITY 14

Work with a partner to think of possible analogies for the following situations. Look at the example, then practise telling each other analogies in complete sentences.

Example: 1. What's wrong with ordering water at a Tim Hortons restaurant?

> Ordering water at Tim Hortons is like going to a steak restaurant and ordering the vegetarian meal.

1. What does it feel like when you have too much homework?
2. Describe the experience of winning first prize.
3. How does it feel to accomplish a goal you had set for yourself?
4. Explain what it is like to learn English as a second language.

Speaking STRATEGY 🗩

To the expert, all details and descriptions seem important, but for new learners, jargon (words very specific to a subject) and small details can quickly become overwhelming, so it is best to stick to the main ideas, and leave the finer details for later.

🛉🛉🛉 SPEAKING ACTIVITY 15

Share anecdotes with a partner, using the following situations to get you started. Your anecdote may be true or made up.

1. learning to ride a bicycle
2. cooking for yourself for the first time
3. going to a restaurant when you didn't speak the same language as the server
4. travelling by yourself
5. meeting new friends
6. missing a homework deadline
7. helping a friend in need
8. volunteering
9. getting caught telling a lie
10. other: _____

🛉 SPEAKING ACTIVITY 16

Choose one of the following complex situations and prepare an explanation using analogies and anecdotes. Practise your explanation, then present it to the class.

1. You have to explain to your grandmother what Facebook is.
2. You want to show your parents how to use Twitter.
3. Use your personal knowledge and teach your group something you have learned: for example, how an engine works, how to buy a car, how to prepare for a job interview, how to get to the local mall.

Speaking STRATEGY 🗩

When introducing a new idea or explaining a new concept to someone, leave certain new information out of the explanation as this can easily be revisited once the learner has a better understanding.

PRONUNCIATION

Pronunciation Focus 1: Applying Common Contractions

Contractions are frequently used in natural speaking and rarely used in formal writing. One or two letters are removed to join two words together.

Some Common Contractions in Spoken English

Positive Forms			
I am > I'm	I have > I've	I will > I'll	I would > I'd
you are > you're	you have > you've	you will > you'll	you would > you'd
he is > he's	he has > he's	he will > he'll	he would > he'd
she is > she's	she has > she's	she will > she'll	she would > she'd
it is > it's	it has > it's	it will > it'll	it would > it'd

John is > John's	John has > John's	John will > John'll	John would > John'd
this is > this's	this has > this's	this will > this'll	this would > this'd
that is > that's	that has > that's	that will > that'll	that would > that'd
we are > we're	we have > we've	we will > we'll	we would > we'd
they are > they're	they have > they've	they will > they'll	they would > they'd
Negative Forms			
is not > isn't are not > aren't was not > wasn't	have not > haven't has not > hasn't	will not > won't	cannot > can't would not > wouldn't

👥 PRONUNCIATION ACTIVITY 1

Listen to the following sentences that contain contractions, then with your partner practise saying each sentence out loud.

 **Track 60**

1. Don't ask me how old I am because I won't tell you.
2. She's much nicer when she hasn't missed her breakfast.
3. We would've finished if you'd given us more time.
4. That's what you think, isn't it?
5. She's almost finished and you haven't started.

👥 PRONUNCIATION ACTIVITY 2

Listen to this dialogue, then assign roles and practise the dialogue with a partner.

 **Track 61**

Situation: Steve can't go to the game.

Sam: Hey, Steve. Can you come to the game tonight?

Steve: I can't. I've got to stay home tonight. I'd rather go out with you guys though.

Sam: It's okay. Don't worry.

Steve: Yeah, Susie'd kill me. She's been planning this dinner for weeks.

Sam: Yeah, I know you'd come if you could, but you can't. It's okay—I'd do the same.

Steve: I'm free on Friday though. Didn't you say there'd be a game on Friday, too?

Sam: Sure, I'll call you.

Steve: Thanks, don't forget, 'cause I'd really like to watch the game with you guys.

👥 PRONUNCIATION ACTIVITY 3

Make up your own dialogue with a partner using as many contractions as you can. When you are ready, demonstrate your dialogue to another pair.

Pronunciation Focus 2: Applying Fast Speech Strategies

Achieving native speaker–like fluency often involves deleting or altering sounds. There are a number of rules of thumb that can help speakers improve the smoothness of their speech.

1. Many vowel sounds are deleted in common usage:

   Niagara, camera, laboratory, temperature

2. When the letter **h** is at the beginning of **un**stressed syllables, it is often deleted if it follows a consonant.

   I have his books.

   I need her to work tomorrow.

3. The sounds / t / and / d / are often deleted or altered.

   - When the letters **t** and **d** appear between two consonant sounds—particularly after the sound / n /—they are deleted:

     international, best friend, bandwidth

   - When the sound / t / appears between vowel sounds and is **not** stressed, the sound is typically pronounced like the sound / d /.

     The / t / sound is unstressed here, so the /t/ sound is pronounced / d /:

     butter, litre, pity, Italy, united

     The / t / sound is stressed here, so the / t / sound is pronounced / t /:

     Italian, eighteen

   - If the sound / t / is followed by the letter **y**, the two sounds merge to sound like / tʃ / (as in **ch**ip):

     can't you, won't you, wouldn't you

   - If the sound / d / is followed by the letter **y**, the two sounds merge to sound like / dʒ / (as in **j**udge):

     did you, would you, could you

👥 PRONUNCIATION ACTIVITY 4

Track 62

A. Listen carefully to the words and strike through the deleted sound in each one.

   Example: Niaga̶ra

   different   average   family   coverage   laboratory   favourite
   chocolate   vegetable   listening   _____   _____   _____

B. Work with your class to add more words to the list. Then practise saying all of them out loud with your partner.

PRONUNCIATION ACTIVITY 5

Track 63

A. Listen to each sentence, then repeat. With a partner, practise saying the sentences again, without enunciating the underlined final / t /, final / d /, and initial / h / (unstressed) sounds.

1. Han<u>d</u> me the papers.
2. Sen<u>d</u> me some money.
3. I wan<u>t</u> more sleep.
4. We los<u>t</u> time there.
5. Give <u>h</u>im the books.
6. They asked <u>h</u>er to respond.
7. Has <u>h</u>e finished yet?
8. Did <u>h</u>is friend go?

B. Now add four more sentences with final / t /, final / d /, and initial / h / sound deletions for your partner to read aloud to you.

1. _____
2. _____
3. _____
4. _____

PRONUNCIATION ACTIVITY 6

Track 64

Listen to these sentences, then take turns with a partner reading the sentences as you heard them, without the / t / and / d / sounds.

It raine<u>d</u> today, but my ol<u>d</u> car kep<u>t</u> going.

My ol<u>d</u> boyfriend's on the nex<u>t</u> bus.

I ate twen<u>ty</u> san<u>d</u>wiches las<u>t</u> night.

Her gran<u>d</u>son Jorge is her mos<u>t</u> travelled gran<u>d</u>child.

Don'<u>t</u> ask me to fin<u>d</u> his keys again.

PRONUNCIATION ACTIVITY 7

Track 65

Review Rule 3 on page 144, then listen to the dialogue and practise saying it with a partner.

Aubrey: Did you see my new car?

Bailey: No, what did you get?

Aubrey: Could you come over? I'll show you.

Bailey: Can't you just tell me? I don't want to go all the way over there.

Aubrey: Alright, but could you keep it a secret? I want to tell ChoCho myself.

Bailey: Didn't you tell her? Well, she's going to love it. Anyway . . .

Aubrey: Yeah, it's a 2014 Beamer.

👥 PRONUNCIATION ACTIVITY 8

In groups of three, sit in circles and take turns making sentences with the patterns that are started for you below. Keep making sentences until your teacher tells you to switch patterns. Continue until each of the group members has made several sentences for each pattern.

Pattern 1. *gotta* (got to)	Pattern 2. *useta* (used to)
Person A: I've *gotta* go. Person B: I've *gotta* eat. Person C: I've *gotta* study harder. Person A: I've *gotta* make another sentence. . . .	Person A. I *useta* be thin. Person B. I *useta* like doughnuts. Person C. I *useta* live in Hamilton. Person A. I *useta* play Pong. . . .
Pattern 3. *coulda* (could have)	**Pattern 4. *don' wanna* (don't want to)**
Person A. I *coulda* been a star. Person B. I *coulda* won. Person C. I *coulda* slept in. Person A. I *coulda* answered better. . . .	Person A. I *don' wanna* stop. Person B. I *don' wanna* take the test next week. Person C. I *don' wanna* miss lunch. Person A. I *don' wanna* shout. . . .

👥 PRONUNCIATION ACTIVITY 9

Create four or five of your own sentences like those in the activities above. Then, build a dialogue with your partner in which you ask questions to elicit these types of responses. Respond to your partner's sentences using a natural and smooth speaking voice.

Hint: Use the answer plus comment or question technique:

Sue: How are you doing?

John: I'm doing well (answer); I really wanna get a good job though. (plus comment)

Sue: Where are you looking? Have you tried the job bank?

John: I useta to use that (answer); do you recommend it? (plus question)

COMMUNICATING IN THE REAL WORLD

Work in groups of three to four to create and showcase a panel discussion in front of the class. First, within your group, choose a topic that you find interesting and have some background knowledge about. Then decide on a moderator (see Communication Focus 3) with the rest of your group as panellists.

Moderator: Using strategies from Communication Focus 1, prepare an introduction of the topic, a short introduction for each of the "expert" panellists, and a "grabber" that would get the audience interested.

Panellists: Each panellist will be role-playing an expert of some kind on the topic the group has chosen. Choose your particular point of view on the topic, and then brainstorm ideas that will support your perspective as an expert on the topic. When presenting your ideas during the panel discussion, remember to do your best to incorporate various degrees of certainty as practised in Communication Focus 2 and explain ideas using strategies from Communication Focus 4.

SELF-EVALUATION

Think about your work in this chapter. For each row in the chart sections **Grammar and Language Functions**, **Pronunciation**, **Learning Strategies**, and **Note-Taking**, give yourself a score based on the rating scale below and write a comment in the Notes section.

Show the chart to your teacher. Talk about what you need to do to make your English better.

Rating Scale

1	2	3	4	5

Needs improvement. ←——————————————→ *Great!*

	Score	Notes
Grammar and Language Functions		
beginning a group presentation		
participating in a panel discussion		
expressing degrees of certainty		
moderating a panel discussion		
using the subjunctive mood		
explaining complex ideas		

Pronunciation

applying common contractions		
applying fast speech strategies		

Learning Strategies

Speaking

building social networks		
maintaining a neutral position		
using anecdotes to add a personal touch		

Listening

visualizing mind maps		
anticipating answers and questions		

Note-Taking

developing a mind map for a panel discussion		
preparing a notes chart for interviews		

Vocabulary and Language Chunks

Look at this list of new vocabulary and language chunks you learned in this chapter. Give yourself a score based on the rating scale and write a comment.

hurdle	consequently	point (sth) out	make history
primary	bias	take note of sth	rising through the
media coverage	to benefit others	to better sth	ranks
corruption	editor-in-chief (EIC)	carry on (and on)	top job
state intervention	day one-er	have access to sth	a move in the right
maladministration	male-dominated	play an important role	direction
media	pushy	no matter what	take s/o by surprise
element	bossy	(s/o says)	is ascribed to
repercussions	code	bring sth to s/o's	time of flux
consequences	columnist	attention	right on
poverty	distinguished	the ultimate (person,	weigh on one's mind
devastation	scrutiny	thing)	pull himself up by his
notion	gender		bootstraps
	uncertainty		take a gamble
	downside		ragtag

	Score	Notes
understanding new vocabulary and language chunks		
using new lexical items freely and confidently		

My plan for practising is _____

_____

_____

CHAPTER 6

Social Change

Synthesizing content from multiple sources

Using rhetorical language

Managing a seminar

THINKING AND TALKING

With your partner, brainstorm activities that you can do that result in a product: for example, knitting, drawing, sculpting, woodworking, etc. Discuss the benefits of these activities to society and on our environment.

LISTENING 1

Before You Listen

👥 PRE-LISTENING ACTIVITY 1

With a partner, decide on one of the three initiatives below to research. Do a quick Google search to get a general idea about your choice, and report to the class what you have learned.

1. Me to We
2. Be World Ready
3. Volunteering opportunities at your own school

👥 PRE-LISTENING ACTIVITY 2

Some lecturers, in delivering a presentation, will follow a very clear IBC (introduction, body, conclusion) structure, while others move from point to point with anecdotes and examples before returning to the main idea. With your partner, review the chart of common organizational words and phrases below and add as many more of your own as you can.

to change direction	to add information	to qualify	to organize	to exemplify
however	moreover	sometimes	so	for example
on the other hand	furthermore	often	first	that is to say
not to mention (that)		never	second	what I mean is
		rarely	next	in other words

UPFRONT VOCABULARY

activism — the act of working to achieve political or social change

clicktivism — (*click* + *activism*) the use of social media and other online methods to promote a political or social cause

craft (n.)	an activity involving a special skill at making things with your hands*
craft (v.)	to make sth using special skills, especially with your hands*
craftivist	(*craft + activist*) a person who crafts in order to work on achieving political or social change
MP	Member of Parliament—a government official
slacktivism	(*slack + activism*) actions performed via the Internet in support of a political or social cause but regarded as requiring little time or involvement, for example, signing an online petition or joining a campaign group on a social media website

*Definition courtesy of *Oxford Advanced Learner's Dictionary.*

🎧 PRE-LISTENING VOCABULARY

Read the following sentences. The underlined words are vocabulary that you will hear in the lecture. On each blank, write a synonym for the underlined word or phrase, using context clues to help you understand its meaning. When you have finished, work with a partner to create your own sentences using the same vocabulary.

Listening STRATEGY 🎧

Listen for emphasized examples, definitions, and quotes—items that are given extra stress, a higher pitch, or more volume. These words usually carry the most meaning.

Speakers may also spell out important words or accompany important information with body language.

Synonym:

_____ Studying a language is so <u>draining</u>; I need to use my brain constantly. I am feeling completely <u>drained</u> by the end of the week, so the weekend is refreshing.

_____ I have to <u>do loads of</u> homework almost every night. It is a lot of work for me.

_____ My goal is to use English for every aspect of my life so it becomes my <u>default</u> language and I no longer need to think about trying to use it with my friends.

_____ I am conscious of the fact that using my own first language will alienate me from anyone who doesn't speak it. Doing this will never help me <u>fit in</u> with them.

_____ Handkerchiefs are handy pieces of cloth that can be used to wipe away tears or perspiration on very hot days. My <u>hanky</u> came in very handy on my wedding day.

1. _____ Last time I played hide-and-go-seek, I needed to use my hanky <u>to blow</u>[1] my nose, but I didn't want <u>to blow</u>[2] my secret location with all that noise.

2. _____

_____   My classmate is a <u>critical friend</u> to have because I know I can trust her, and she will be completely honest with me.

_____   I would like English to be a part of my everyday life, not sth I <u>opt into</u> just once in a while.

Note-Taking

 **Track 66**

Sarah Corbett leads the "Craftivist Collective," a small group of people who use their original and inspiring art to challenge people's views of the world. She explains how voicing your opinion through creativity can make your voice stronger and your compassion deeper.

Listen to the lecture "A Craftivist Story" for the first time and use the organizational cue Sarah gives in the introduction ("Today, I want to talk to you about three problems I've found to be . . .") to create a framework for your notes.

Decide which note-taking style you want to use, either the mind-mapping style or the listing style, and leave spaces after each main idea so you can add more information later. Listen for speaker emphasis as described in the listening strategy to help you find main ideas and key information to write in your notes. When you are finished, compare your notes with those of a classmate by asking each other questions regarding main ideas and information you missed, and add to your notes.

Listening for the Main Ideas

 Track 67

Listen to the lecture "A Craftivist Story" again and add details to each of the main ideas in your notes. After listening, use your notes to answer the questions, and compare answers with a partner.

1. What were the main ideas that Sarah focused on in her speech regarding traditional forms of activism?
2. What is the "tool" that Sarah says saved her?
3. Summarize the most important aspects of Sarah's talk in three or four sentences.

Listening Comprehension

 Track 68

Listen to the lecture again and answer the questions.

1. Crafting led Sarah to accomplish several things related to justice issues. List two of them.
2. Why did Sarah's MP tell her to stop emailing her?
3. What did Sarah do to build a relationship with her MP?
4. What can craft do to promote a cause without being negative?

5. List all the activist stereotypes that Sarah mentions to explain why she doesn't fit in with traditional activists.

6. According to Sarah, how is crafting on one's own or in small groups more positive than the traditional activist way of promoting change?

7. What three social networking tools does Sarah mention that people use to promote activism to the rest of the world?

Personalizing

Sarah feels as though being a craftivist helps her be a better person, and in the audio, she encourages her listeners to "be the best [people] they can be." Follow Sarah's advice by working in groups of three and following the four steps outlined below.

1. Make a list of causes that interest your group.

2. Choose one of the causes from your list that you are all interested in.

3. Prepare a proposal for an event that would help promote your cause in a positive way.

4. Share your project proposal with the whole class.

Extension activity: Choose the class's best proposal and activate it outside of class.

Vocabulary and Language Chunks

Work with a partner and a dictionary to learn the meaning of the vocabulary and language chunks below. Then, prepare a dialogue with a partner using as much of the new language as you can. When you have practised your dialogue, perform it for the class.

1. messed up
2. justice issues
3. be part of the solution
4. talking at s/o (different from talking to s/o)
5. thread through my life
6. half the time we . . .
7. take ownership of sth
8. to be in a bubble

SPEAKING 1

Communication Focus 1:
Synthesizing Content from Multiple Sources

A convincing speaker is able to show a clear connection between content and knowledge. To support a point of view, a speaker paraphrases and summarizes what has been said or written by content experts, then synthesizes by including points from those sources. The synthesis may include some of the speaker's own knowledge.

1. We can support an argument by restating the original point or argument.

   These expressions are useful:

   In other words . . .

   Let me explain . . .

   What she/he means to say is (that) . . .

2. We can support an argument by restating its most important or key elements.

   These expressions are useful:

   In brief . . .

   In a nutshell . . .

   To sum up . . .

3. We can support an argument by comparing and combining multiple sources of information with previous knowledge; this is called synthesizing.

   Often these kinds of expressions are used:

   Over time . . .

   The impact has been . . .

   . . . combined with . . .

   . . . has changed from . . . to . . .

   . . . compares to . . .

   . . . is different from . . .

   At first I thought . . ., but now I believe/understand that . . .

   (And) I'd like to add that . . .

   I'd take that a step further . . .

Grammar Note: Reporting Speech—Questions and Commands

Reporting what others have said or written is an important part of the process of synthesizing. Remember that in reporting what someone has said, certain changes take place (changes in tense and pronouns—see Chapter 2). When restating questions and commands, there are some further grammatical details to focus on.

1. For questions, note that the subject comes before the verb and it is not necessary to use **do** or **did**.

   Examples:

   "What time does the lesson start?" → She asked what time the lesson started.

   "Where did Wisteria go?" → She asked where Wisteria went.

2. For commands, note that the structure is ***told/commanded*** + name/ pronoun + the infinitive of the verb. The verbs ***told*** or ***commanded*** are used instead of the verb ***said***.

Examples:

David said to Lucy:
"Close the door!" → David <u>told Lucy to close</u> the door.

→ David <u>commanded Lucy to close</u> the door.

→ He <u>commanded her to close</u> the door.

Elaine said to the kids:
"Run away!" → Elaine <u>told the kids to run away</u>.

→ Elaine <u>commanded them to run away</u>.

→ She <u>commanded the kids to run away</u>.

👥 **SPEAKING ACTIVITY 1**

For each quote from the list, report to your partner what the speaker said by paraphrasing his or her words and synthesizing by adding your own perspective to the speaker's ideas.

Speaking STRATEGY 💬

Paraphrasing or summarizing information is a good way to start a formal or academic conversation.

Example:

The duty of youth is to challenge corruption. —Kurt Cobain

→ Kurt Cobain has argued that young people have to confront things that are unfair in the world, and I would add that his work with young people was highly recognized.

1. A small group of thoughtful committed citizens can change the world. —Margaret Mead

2. A change is brought about because ordinary people do extraordinary things. —Barack Obama

3. Get up, stand up. Stand up for your rights. —Bob Marley

4. Unless someone like you cares a whole awful lot, nothing is going to get better. It's not. —Dr. Seuss

5. Say what you want, but you never say it with violence. —Gerard Way

6. If you don't like the news, go out and make some of your own. —Wes Nisker

7. I have two parallel things I'm interested in. One is, I'm interested in collecting interesting stories, and the other is I'm interested in collecting interesting research. What I'm looking for is cases where they overlap. —Malcolm Gladwell

8. What are you doing for others? —Martin Luther King

9. It is not enough to be busy. The question is, what are we busy about? —Henry David Thoreau

10. Do we make history or does history make us? —Salman Rushdie

ⁿⁿⁿ SPEAKING ACTIVITY 2

Work in groups of three. One person at a time opens the book and reports pieces of information from the list below by whispering facts to one partner who will then report that information to the next. Continue until each of you has shared and reported at least three pieces of information.

Facts about Poverty in Canada

15 percent of Canadians have low income —Statistics Canada	Poverty has been steadily rising in Canada since the 1990s —Statistics Canada	13 percent of Canadian children live in poverty —UNICEF
There is a 21-year gap in life expectancy between Hamilton's richest and poorest neighbourhoods —*Hamilton Spectator*	900,000 Canadians are assisted by food banks each month —Food Banks Canada	38 percent of those assisted by food banks in Canada are children or youth —Food Banks Canada
As many as 200,000 Canadians experience homelessness each year —Canadian Homelessness Research Network	On any given night, 30,000 Canadians are homeless —Canadian Homelessness Research Network	The average Canadian owes $1.63 for every dollar they earn —Statistics Canada
Poverty costs Ontario approximately 6 percent of its GDP —Ontario Association of Food Banks	National healthcare costs related to poverty are estimated at $7.6 billion —Ontario Association of Food Banks	Every dollar invested in child poverty now saves $3–9 in future spending on the health and criminal justice systems —Public Health Agency of Canada

(Source: Adapted from information on the CBC website: http://www.cbc.ca/strombo/news/10-things-you-might-not-know-about-poverty-in-canada, 17 October 2013.)

Example:

Jules whispers to Kelly: "Toronto is much larger than Ottawa."

Pat: [to Kelly] What did Jules say?

Kelly: [to Pat] Jules said that Toronto was much larger than Ottawa.

Kelly whispers to Pat: "Canada has a population of less than 35,000,000 people."

Jules: [to Pat] What did Kelly say?

Pat: [to Jules] Kelly said that . . .

👥 SPEAKING ACTIVITY 3

Create a dialogue with your partner about what you did yesterday and practise it out loud. When you are ready, perform it for your group. As pairs present dialogues, group members practise interrupting and asking for repetition.

Example:

> Taylor: Hi, Jennifer, how are you?
> Group: What did Taylor say?
> Jennifer: Taylor said hello and asked me how I am.
>
> Jennifer: I'm great, thanks for asking. What did you do yesterday?
> Group: Taylor, what did Jennifer ask you?
> Taylor: She asked me what I did yesterday.
>
> . . .

👥 SPEAKING ACTIVITY 4

With your partner, study the population chart below and what information can be synthesized from the facts shown.

Montreal and Toronto—Population Growth

Population	Montreal (CMA*)	Toronto (CMA)
1961	2,110,679	1,919,000
1971	2,743,208	2,628,045
1981	2,862,286	2,998,947
1991	3,127,242	3,893,933
2001	3,426,350	4,682,897
2011	3,824,221	5,583,064
*CMA: Census Metropolitan Area		

(Source: Wikipedia.)

Montreal has dropped from being Canada's most populated city to second-most.

Over 55 years Toronto's population has increased more significantly than Montreal's.

Toronto's population has grown from 1.9 million to over five and a half million.

Combine the information from each pair of two separate events that have common themes:

1. Describe your last two weekends, synthesizing information about both.
2. Describe your travel experiences, synthesizing information about your last two trips.

3. Explain what you have learned as a student at your present institution. Synthesize experiences from your history there.

4. Describe how you have grown by synthesizing achievements and experiences both in school and outside of school.

👥 SPEAKING ACTIVITY 5

Consider the statements in the synthesis chart below. Record your original thoughts, then discuss the statements and your own original ideas with a partner. Record your partner's thoughts. After your discussion, record in the synthesis column any revised thoughts and new understanding you now have based on your discussion. When your chart is complete, discuss with your partner what, if anything, made you change your views.

Statements	Original Thoughts	Partner's Thoughts	Synthesis
Vegetarians are healthier than people who eat meat.			
The Canadian government should add historically significant women to its bank notes.			
If you see a pet locked in a stranger's car on a hot day, it's okay to break the car window.			

👥 SPEAKING ACTIVITY 6

Think of a slang expression or word. Find a definition for the word or phrase in at least two different dictionaries, including a slang dictionary. Synthesize the information you gather and explain the different meanings of the word to your class.

Example:

cool

Dictionary 1:

cool (adjective; slang)

wonderful, excellent; acceptable

popular, fashionable: "I love your new car, it's so cool!"

Dictionary 2:

cool (adj; informal)

1. /kul/ [-er/-est] used to show approval: "Is it cool to invite Sue?" "Sure, that's cool."

2. /kul/ [-er/-est] wonderful, excellent: "It's cool that you showed up—thanks!"

SPEAKING ACTIVITY 7

Prepare five questions about one current world event. Design each question so that you will be able to elicit (get) an opinion. Ask five of your classmates, one at a time, your prepared questions. Take notes regarding the similarities and differences in answers you receive from your classmates. When you are finished, use your notes to prepare a summary and synthesis of your findings to present to the class.

Sample topics:

How do greenhouse gases harm the environment?

What can be done to eliminate poverty?

How can we help the homeless?

LISTENING 2

Before You Listen

PRE-LISTENING ACTIVITY 1

Work with a partner and add as many possible uses of the Internet and social networking tools like Facebook, Twitter, etc. to the list. Then, synthesize your list with your classmates' lists.

	Done	Haven't Done	Tools Used
research			
meet people			
collaborate on a project online			
inform people in your own network of what you are doing (status update)			
organize an event			

👪 PRE-LISTENING ACTIVITY 2

A petition is a request for change supported by people's signatures and presented to a person in power. Have you ever received a request to sign an online petition? Have you ever signed one? Have you clicked the "like" button for a social cause online? Do you think signing online petitions can create real change in the world? Choose a cause from the list below (or one of your own) that you could get your whole class to sign a petition on, and discuss the issues surrounding that cause.

Sample causes:

petition teacher to change the due date of an assignment

petition classmates to use only English during class time

petition student union to organize a campus ban on plastic bottles

other _____

UPFRONT VOCABULARY

hooking up	(*informal*) to meet sb and spend time with them*
platform	the aims of a political party and the things they say they will do if they are elected*
forge	to put a lot of effort into making sth successful or strong so that it will last*
sniper	a person who shoots at sb from a hidden position*
triangulate	finding out position and location by measuring the distance between two fixed points and then measuring the angle from each of these to the third point*
makeshift	used temporarily for a particular purpose because the real thing is not available*
wiki	a website that allows any user to change or add to the information it contains*
wikinomics	(*wiki + economics*) the use of mass collaboration in a business environment

*Definition courtesy of *Oxford Advanced Learner's Dictionary.*

👥 PRE-LISTENING VOCABULARY

Choose one of the lists below (your partner chooses the other) and use your dictionary to find the meanings of the words. Share your findings by explaining the words to each other.

List 1	List 2
kinda	strong ties
revolutionary	incubate
online community	take s/o out
weak ties	treat as subjects
sth is underway	community

Note-Taking

Don Tapscott is a famous Canadian author and a leader in exploring the impact that social media and the Internet have on society and the world. Some of his books include *Growing Up Digital: The Rise of the Net Generation, Wikinomics: How Mass Collaboration Changes Everything,* and *Macrowikinomics: Rebooting Business and the World.*

In the lecture that you will hear Don Tapscott give, he explains the impact of social media on self-organization. He refers to how, in one day, his son developed an online community of 130 members in seven countries. He gives another example, illustrating how revolutionaries in Tunisia and Syria used social media on the battleground.

Listen to the lecture "Social Sciences and Social Change in the Age of Social Media" for the first time and count (using check marks ✓) the instances of each of the emphatic strategies that the speaker uses.

- repeating information   _____
- paraphrasing information   _____
- tone (changing the sound of voice, louder, quieter)   _____
- reference to a picture, book, quote, related issue, or other reading   _____

Note: When you can see the speaker, the following emphatic strategies are also worth taking note of.

- body language
- writing on the board
- diagrams, graphs, illustrations, pictures

Listening STRATEGY

Asking yourself critical questions about the content of the lecture helps keep your mind engaged and focused on the content all the while developing a deeper understanding of what you hear. While listening, ask:

1. What do I know about this topic already?
2. Do I agree with the speaker? Why, why not?
3. How does my prior knowledge (textbook/ other source) fit with what I am hearing now?

Listening for the Main Ideas

Listen to "Social Sciences and Social Change in the Age of Social Media" again, and on a separate piece of paper, write down only the information that the speaker emphasizes. (See the Listening Strategy earlier in this chapter regarding stress, higher pitch, and volume.)

At the beginning of the audio clip we hear, "but social networking is becoming social **production**, it's not just hooking up online"—so you write *production* in your notes.

Note how recognizing the significance of the emphasized word *production* helps you answer the question "What is social networking becoming?"

When you have finished recording the emphasized words on your paper, use your notes to answer the questions.

1. What is social production?
2. According to Tapscott, what is **not** an example of social production?
3. What is self-organization?
4. How is self-organization different today from 100 years ago?

Listening Comprehension

 **Track 71**   Read the questions about "Social Sciences and Social Change in the Age of Social Media." Listen to the lecture again, and answer the questions. Check your answers with your partner.

1. What does Tapscott refer to when he states that it has been produced socially, is 10–20 times bigger than *Encyclopaedia Britannica,* is in over 200 different languages, is just as accurate, and is not owned by anyone?

2. Tapscott relates a personal anecdote about giving his book *Wikinomics* to his son on Christmas Day. Why did he share that anecdote?

3. What are two historical examples of self-organization that Tapscott mentions?

4. Tapscott refers to Malcolm Gladwell, who used the term *slacktivists.* Whom is Gladwell talking about?

5. Tapscott refers to conflicts in Tunisia and Syria in his lecture. What does he want to illustrate with these examples?

Personalizing

Have you ever used your social networking tools (Facebook, Twitter, Instagram, etc.) to organize a successful social event? Work in small groups to design and carry out a social event of your choice that also includes friends and/ or family members who will participate via the Internet. Consider issues like language barriers and time differences in your planning.

Here are some sample ideas:

conversation practice around the world

a virtual social gathering of friends from around the world

raising awareness with people from around the world for a specific cause

Vocabulary and Language Chunks

Use the context clues from Don Tapscott's lecture to gain understanding of the following language chunks. Write a synonym or definition in your own words, then check your answers with those of a classmate.

Context Clues	Synonyms or Definitions
The quality (of Wikipedia) is **just as good** (as *Britannica*) but nobody owns it.	

What used to **take place** over a long time can now happen really fast.

_____

Obama thinks my book *Wikinomics* is the key to winning an election and my reaction was "**I am the man**."

_____

But **not so fast**; as it turns out, I was not the only one who contributed to Obama winning his election.

_____

Real change **comes about** through major events that occur.

_____

The relationship between a mother and her baby is strong **from the get-go**.

_____

You can **say what you want** about sth, but it won't change the facts.

_____

SPEAKING 2

Communication Focus 2: Using Rhetorical Language

Speakers use rhetorical language to create more interesting or persuasive arguments and to help the listener make a strong connection to the content. In Chapter 5, you learned about analogies and anecdotes, which are common rhetorical devices. Here are some more commonly used rhetorical devices.

Rhetorical Device	Function
a. analogy	points out a similar characteristic between two very different things
b. allusion	an indirect reference to a person or subject, often from pop culture
c. hyperbole	an exaggeration
d. oxymoron	a two-word paradox
e. parallelism	uses words or phrases with a repetitive grammatical structure
f. rhetorical question	a question used to draw the listener's attention, and no answer is expected
g. understatement	makes an idea seem less important/serious than it really is

👥 SPEAKING ACTIVITY 8

Work with a partner and match the following sentences with their rhetorical devices by writing the corresponding letter from the chart above.

1. ___ I got 10 out of 10 on my last vocabulary test; that's not bad, I think.
2. ___ Did he (Obama) change the way we govern?
3. ___ This jumbo shrimp is pretty ugly.
4. ___ I like my coffee black as hell, but sweet as heaven.
5. ___ I don't like dressing up. I don't like shouting . . .
6. ___ So, who's the new Einstein in class?
7. ___ I've been to Niagara Falls a thousand times.

👥 SPEAKING ACTIVITY 9

Working with a partner, read the examples of rhetorical speech below to help you, then make your own sentences. Take turns: Student A suggests a type of rhetoric; Student B makes a sentence; then partners switch.

Rhetorical Device	Example
analogy	Human memory is like a computer: long-term memory is the hard drive that stores data, and short-term memory is like RAM, which is only there while you are using it.
allusion	You should have seen him skate—he thought he was Gretzky out there.
hyperbole	I worked so hard on the campaign, I can't even lift a finger.
parallelism	The voters were loud, and the voters were opinionated, but ultimately, the voters were ours.
rhetorical question	Do you think we organized this event for our own benefit?
understatement	He said we wouldn't get 1,000 participants at the rally; we got 3,500. Not too bad, eh?

SPEAKING ACTIVITY 10

Work in groups of four and practise saying sentences of different rhetorical functions while your group members use the cards handed out in class to match the correct rhetorical function you are using.

SPEAKING ACTIVITY 11

Discuss with your group which rhetorical devices you feel most comfortable using, and why. What are some of the situations where you could use these devices effectively?

SPEAKING ACTIVITY 12

With your partner, list all of the idioms and expressions you know that use "as . . . as . . . ." You may start with ones that have animals in them.

Examples:

> **as sly as a fox, as busy as a bee**

SPEAKING ACTIVITY 13

Develop a short speech about your hometown. Try to employ enough rhetorical devices to make your speech sound emotional and convincing (from your heart). When you are ready, share speeches with your partner.

Communication Focus 3: Managing a Seminar

Leading and managing a seminar is an opportunity to express ideas and expertise about a topic. It serves as a chance for participants to contribute to a knowledge base. Seminar leaders must be prepared to engage participants, speak effectively, and listen carefully, in order to paraphrase participants' comments and summarize and synthesize the discussions of the seminar.

SPEAKING ACTIVITY 14

In groups, discuss the effectiveness of the following ways to engage participants in a seminar. Reflect on your own experiences in group work and seminars. After your discussion, work with your group to itemize which three are the most important. Explain your choices.

____	get to know participants' names	____	use humour
____	use an icebreaker to get started	____	use eye contact
____	speak positively; thank and compliment participants	____	move around the room
____	stay on track	____	use pictures/video for variety
____	know when to stop talking and when to move on	____	use PowerPoint, KeyNote, or Prezi
____	give tasks that are manageable and allow for participant control		

🏃🏃 SPEAKING ACTIVITY 15

Tone of voice is a major factor in first impressions, and on the phone in particular, it can be misinterpreted. Note that tone often exposes a speaker's emotions or mood—the same words could have two completely different meanings:

> **Teacher: Tomorrow's class is cancelled.**
>
> **Student: That's great.**

Both the teacher's and student's tone could show either enthusiasm or sarcasm and disgust.

Track 72

Listen to the following sentences and repeat them by mimicking the exact tone of the speaker. Discuss with your partner how the intended meaning of the sentences changes because of tone. Then practise changing the intention of each sentence by using a different tone with it.

Speaking STRATEGY 💬

Control your tone of voice to express your emotions effectively, passionately, enthusiastically—or to conceal them.

1. Good morning. (happy)
2. Thank you. (ironic)
3. That's a great idea. (enthusiastic)
4. I feel great. (sad)
5. I have got to go. (angry)

🏃🏃🏃 SPEAKING ACTIVITY 16

An important part of introducing a topic for a seminar is to offer an appropriate and clear initial statement of your position. Work with a partner and ask the question: "What is one thing that you believe is true and that you wish to argue?" about each of the topics in the list below. Then, write your answer, **your position**, in the space provided.

Example:

Topics:	Position:
bicycle helmets	**Citizens in a free country must be free to choose whether they want to wear a bicycle helmet or not.**

women's rights   _____

racial issues   _____

legal driving age   _____

legal drinking age   _____

use of social media   _____

Facebook "friending"   _____
a teacher

other: _____   _____

🏃🏃 SPEAKING ACTIVITY 17

Work with a partner. Take one of the topics and a position from Speaking Activity 16. Then, use the language below to organize an introduction of your topic.

Today, we will learn (about) . . .

Let me explain how . . .

I have some questions for you about . . .

It is important to know how . . .

The issue is . . .

👥 **SPEAKING ACTIVITY 18**

The **discussion** is the main part of a seminar presentation. Work with a partner and practise asking the two types of questions outlined below about the topics in Speaking Activity 17.

Basic Questions	Deeper Questions
What do you think about _____? [situation]	Now that we understand it from Susan's point of view, how would Roslyn perceive this situation?
How do you feel about _____? [situation]	Why do you hold this point of view?
Why does _____ say [person] _____? [position]	When _____ says _____, [person] [position] what are his/her assumptions?
What is the result of _____? [situation/event]	How could this situation have been avoided? How could this situation have been different?
	How might _____ solve this problem? [event or person]
	How could this _____ be applied in [position or situation] the context of our class/school/city?

Speaking STRATEGY 💬

Seminar leaders manage tasks, questions, answers, and comments from participants. They also ask deeper-level or follow-up questions to help further understanding of the topic.

👥 **SPEAKING ACTIVITY 19**

Work with a partner to create follow-up questions as in the examples below.

Examples:

Where are you from? → What is that city like?
→ Why did you leave?
→ How is it different from here?

Are you on Facebook? → When did you join?
→ What do you think Facebook is good for?
→ What don't you like about Facebook and why?

Have you ever started (or wanted to start) your own business?   →

    →

    →

Are you a member of a social club or organization?   →

    →

    →

Would you be interested in starting a social network?   →

    →

    →

SPEAKING ACTIVITY 20

A presenter needs to remain dynamic while leading a seminar and ensure that all participants are active and focused at all times. Work in small groups and discuss why you are studying English and what you will do with your advanced level of English. Take turns managing transitions between speakers in order to keep all speakers engaged.

Use engaging language such as the following:

- Thank you for that great information, _____.
  [person]

- _____ had a great perspective of _____; can you reiterate
  [person]   [situation]
  what you said earlier?

- That is an interesting difference to what _____ just said. Let's
  [person]
  recap both of these perspectives before we move on.

- What do you think _____ meant by _____?
  [person]   [something]

- Could you clarify what you wanted to say when you told us:
  "_____"?
  [something]

- How does your point of view compare with what _____ said
  [person]
  earlier?

- How does what _____ said compare with/contrast with/
  [person]
  support what _____ said?
  [person]

SPEAKING ACTIVITY 21

Work in groups of four. Each group chooses a topic of common interest and prepares, and then leads, a short seminar using the strategies they've learned, with the rest of the class as participants.

PRONUNCIATION

Pronunciation Focus:
Using Common Intonation Patterns—Part 1

Pitch and intonation refer to the melodic patterns that English speakers use in spoken language. These patterns convey meaning as well as a higher level of fluency.

 **Track 73**

Pitch and Intonation

Pitch is the highness or lowness of a sound as the ear hears it. There are three levels of voice pitch: high (like a siren), mid, and low (like a foghorn).

Intonation is changing pitch—applying patterns of pitch. Airport chimes are a good example of different pitch levels.

👥 PRONUNCIATION ACTIVITY 1

A. Listen to the following examples of sentences (positive and negative statements and information questions) that follow the mid pitch–high pitch–low pitch (/2–3–1/) pattern of intonation.

3	class-
2	He taught in the
1	-room.

3	class-
2	He didn't teach in the
1	-room.

3	come
2	Where does she
1	from?

B. Work with a partner and create a dialogue by asking and answering information questions (ones that begin with a question word). Pay special attention to the /2–3–1/ pattern as you speak. Practise the intonation pattern first with the sample dialogue below.

Example:

> Person A: Where did you go last night?
> Person B: I went to Tim Hortons.
> Person A: Why didn't you go to the office?
> Person B: Because the office was closed.

PRONUNCIATION ACTIVITY 2

A. Yes/no questions follow a different intonation pattern. Listen to the following examples of yes/no questions that follow the /2–3/ pattern of intonation.

3	-late?
2	Do you like choco-
1	

3	long?
2	Have you been here
1	

B. Work with a partner and practise asking and answering the following questions, paying special attention to the /2–3/ pattern as you speak. Add a few more questions of your own.

1. Have you ever completed an online survey?
2. Do you study every day?
3. Would you ever consider becoming a craftivist?
4. Will you read Don Tapscott's *Wikinomics*?
5. Do you know what a slacktivist is?
6. _____
7. _____
8. _____

PRONUNCIATION ACTIVITY 3

A. Listen to these question-and-answer patterns and note how the arrows indicate the change in pitch at the end of the sentence.

1. /2–3–1/   Where is he going?   *Where is he (2) go (3) ing (1)*
2. /2–3/   Are you busy?   *Are you bu (2) sy (3)*
3. /3–2/   I'm busy.   *I'm bu (3) sy (2)*

B. Next, predict the pitch in each phrase from "Social Sciences and Social Change in the Age of Social Media" that you see below and indicate whether it should rise or fall by circling the correct arrow. Compare your answers with those of your partner. Then, practise speaking the excerpts out loud with each other in a natural tone.

Examples:

/2–3–1/   It's not just 1 billion people on Facebook

/2–3–1/ . . . and 200 million on Twitter

/2–3–1/ . . . but social networking is becoming social production

1. so you can produce all kinds of things
2. an encyclopaedia that's 10 to 20 times bigger than *Britannica*
3. What's going on here?
4. Let me explain
5. Can I watch?

C. Listen to the audio again and check your answers.

PRONUNCIATION ACTIVITY 4

Track 76

A. Listen to these complete and incomplete (open) list patterns in the following examples and note how the arrows indicate rising and falling pitch.

Example:

1. **Would you like coffee, tea, or milk? (complete—just three choices are given)**

   He created a presence on Facebook, Twitter, and Reddit.

2. **Would you like coffee, tea, milk . . .? (incomplete—there are more choices unnamed)**

   There are many web browsers including Firefox, Safari, Chrome . . .

B. Then, work with a partner to create and practise speaking your own lists. Be sure to practise both finished and unfinished lists.

PRONUNCIATION ACTIVITY 5

Track 77

A. Listen to the reasons that Sarah Corbett gives in her lecture regarding why she didn't feel like she fitted in with other activists. As you listen, mark at the ends of these sentences taken from the listening whether rising or falling intonation occur.

B. Afterward, practise speaking the list aloud with a partner and adjust your arrows as necessary to make it sound natural.

1. I really didn't feel like I fitted in as an activist.
2. I'm not a natural extrovert.
3. Uhm, hence the nervous laughter . . .
4. I don't always like being around a lot of people.
5. I quite like doing stuff on my own.
6. I don't like dressing up.
7. I don't like shouting.
8. I'm scared of riding a bike.
9. So some activists don't like me there.
10. I'm not vegan.

11. I love fashion.

12. There's lots of reasons why I didn't feel like I fitted in.

C. Listen to Sarah's list again to check your answers.

 **PRONUNCIATION ACTIVITY 6**

Track 78   Practise reading the example dialogues below, then work with your partner, taking turns each stating general facts. As you hear your partner's facts, repeat them with rising intonation to express doubt, and then falling intonation to show agreement/understanding.

Student A: She lives in Toronto.

Student B: She lives in Toronto?

Student B: (I see,) she lives in Toronto.

Student A: Actually, the moon is a balloon.

Student B: (What?!) The moon is a balloon?

PRONUNCIATION ACTIVITY 7

Find a newscast, informational video, lecture, or even a commercial regarding activism or social change. Write a transcription of the first minute of your segment, and indicate the rising and falling intonation patterns on your transcription. Compare transcriptions and patterns with those of your classmates and see if you notice commonalities, then show your teacher your results. Read your transcription to your partner with the same intonation as the original speaker(s).

COMMUNICATING IN THE REAL WORLD

In this chapter, you listened to two lectures about social change. The lectures were organized and delivered in very different styles. Which lecture was easier to follow for you personally? Why do you think this is? Discuss these questions with your classmates and consider how you can use the best aspects of both of the lectures in your own presentation.

Conduct some research and prepare a 10-minute lecture on one of the topics in the list below. Give concrete details and report facts from your research with statistical and graphical support. Include rhetorical language to support/reinforce your own view of the subject.

social change: eating habits

student activism

making a difference in your community

raising awareness for a cause (recycling, water conservation, healthcare, poverty, social inequality)

SELF-EVALUATION

Think about your work in this chapter. For each row in the chart sections **Grammar and Language Functions**, **Pronunciation**, **Learning Strategies**, and **Note-Taking**, give yourself a score based on the rating scale below and write a comment in the Notes section.

Show the chart to your teacher. Talk about what you need to do to make your English better.

Rating Scale

1	2	3	4	5

Needs ⟵————————————⟶ *Great!*
improvement.

	Score	Notes
Grammar and Language Functions		
synthesizing content from multiple sources		
reporting speech—questions and commands		
using rhetorical language		
managing a seminar		
Pronunciation		
using pitch and common intonation patterns		
Learning Strategies		
Speaking		
opening a discussion by briefly paraphrasing or summarizing information		
controlling tone		
adding depth to discussions by asking deeper-level questions		
Listening		
understanding meaning by recognizing emphasis		
asking critical questions while listening, to stay engaged and focused		
Note-Taking		
using organizational cues		
recognizing emphatic strategies		

Vocabulary and Language Chunks
Look at this list of new vocabulary and language chunks you learned in this chapter. Give yourself a score based on the rating scale and write a comment.

activism	platform	messed up	(be) in a bubble
clicktivism	forge	justice issues	just as good as
craft	sniper	(be) part of the	take place
craftivist	triangulate	solution	(be) the man
MP	makeshift	talk at s/o	not so fast
slacktivism	wiki	talk to s/o	(sth) comes about
draining	wikinomics	thread through sth	from the get go
(do) loads of sth	kinda	half the time	say what you want
default	revolutionary	take ownership of sth	
fit in	online community		
hanky (handkerchief)	weak/strong ties		
(to) blow sth	(sth is) underway		
critical friend	incubates		
opt into sth	take (s/o) out		
hooking up	treat as		
	community		

	Score	Notes
understanding new vocabulary and language chunks		
using new lexical items freely and confidently		

My plan for practising is _____

_____

_____

_____

CHAPTER 7

Young People and the Business World

Evaluating arguments

Debating—Presenting arguments

Debating—Presenting counter-arguments

THINKING AND TALKING

Post-secondary institutions support their students by promoting activities which allow students to gain first-hand, real-world experience. List and talk about the opportunities and processes that are available at your institution. Add to your discussion by searching the Internet for definitions and examples of co-ops, internships, field studies, and overseas study programs at your school. Finally, discuss with your group, the value (benefits) of each.

LISTENING 1

Before You Listen

👥 PRE-LISTENING ACTIVITY 1

Work with your partner. Make a list of the advantages and disadvantages of each type of college/university activity given below. Share your list with the class.

local business internship

out-of-town co-op

course-related field study

overseas study program

👥 PRE-LISTENING ACTIVITY 2

Cornell University's SMART (Student Multidisciplinary Applied Research Teams) program of field studies sends teams of three to five students to work with NGOs (non-government organizations) or small, local businesses to meet challenges in countries that are trying to grow their economy. For example, in 2011, a Cornell team helped a South African entrepreneur start a nursery by developing marketing strategies and a business plan.

In teams of three, decide on one type of small business. Consider the issues that this kind of business may face in a growing economy. Discuss how your team could best apply each other's skills to help it. Then, share your ideas with the class.

UPFRONT VOCABULARY

engage s/o (v.)   succeed in attracting and keeping s/o's attention and interest*

entrepreneur	a person who makes money by starting or running businesses*
determinism	the belief that people are not free to choose what they are like or how they behave, because these things are decided by their surroundings, over which they have no control*
emerging	starting to exist; appearing or becoming known
NGO	non-governmental organization (a charity, an association, etc. that is independent of government and business)*
nutrition	the process by which living things receive the food necessary for them to grow and be healthy*

*Definition courtesy of *Oxford Advanced Learner's Dictionary.*

PRE-LISTENING VOCABULARY

Work with your partner and use a dictionary to choose which word of the pair suggested for each key word is its synonym and underline it.

Key Words	Choice A	Choice B
integrated	counted	combined
innovative	intelligent	original
evaluate	judge	count
phenomenal	objective	outstanding
heartland	centre	coastline
sustainable	achievable	maintainable
instability	weakness	security
rapidity	quickness	timelessness
abolish	determine	end
slavery	oppression	labour
bondage	captivity	trust

Note-Taking

In Canada there are high levels of technology and education that further the advancement of Canadian businesses. Many companies in emerging economies around the world run without that support. Cornell University students in the Emerging Markets program join applied research teams not only to gain first-hand experience in economic development, but also to help small businesses in developing countries to meet complex challenges.

 Track 79

Listen to the lecture "Why Small Is Still Beautiful" and pause after each section to reflect on it by answering the question, "What did I learn from that?" Pause the audio clip at the times indicated below and jot down your reflections. When you have listened to the whole lecture one time, share and compare your reflection notes with your partner.

Section 1.   00:00 to 00:58 ("Over the last 10 years . . ." to ". . . with small companies.")

The program at Cornell and engagement

_____

_____

_____

Section 2.   00:58 to 03:53 ("Uhm we then now said . . ." to ". . . throughout the developing world.")

Cornell student involvement

_____

_____

_____

Section 3.   03:53 to 05:06 ("Uhm, there are challenges . . ." to ". . . and getting our students involved into this process.")

Challenges to the program

_____

_____

_____

Section 4.   05:06 to 11:02 (end) ("Now, I wanna close with . . ." to the end)

Why we should care?

_____

_____

_____

Listening for the Main Ideas

 Track 80

Listen to the lecture again, then use your notes to help you answer the four questions in your own words.

1. How has the program been successful?

_____

_____

2. Describe what the student teams do.

_____

_____

3. Why should Cornell students care about the economic development process?

_____

_____

4. Ultimately, who benefits from this program?

_____

_____

Listening Comprehension

Listen to the beginning of the lecture. Choose the best answer to each question.  **Track 81**

1. When did the program start?

   a. 2001

   b. 10 years ago

   c. 2009

2. How many companies has the program worked with?

   a. almost 1,000

   b. 1,000

   c. more than 1,000

3. The program strives to approach entrepreneurs in emerging economies:

   a. directly

   b. indirectly

   c. both directly and indirectly

4. Who does the program engage?

   a. Cornell students

   b. students from Africa

   c. small companies/businesses in emerging economies

   d. all of the above

5. What kind of development is the focus of working with small companies?

   a. educational

   b. social

   c. economic

   d. all of the above

Personalizing

Student participants in Cornell's program bring their overseas experience back to classrooms as case studies. Think of a "life experience" you have had that your classmates could learn from. How would you present it to them? What would you say? How would you organize your report? Take some time to prepare an outline answering these questions, and then present your thoughts to your class.

Vocabulary and Language Chunks

Work with your partner to combine pairs of words and terms to form the language chunks used in the audio clip. When you've finished, practise making sentences with the language chunks. Check with your teacher for accuracy. The first three have been done for you.

do-good	Arab	approach	multi-disciplinary
ideas	study	program	sleeves
flagship	Spring	case	moral
roll up	rapid	change	imperative

Arab Spring

multi-disciplinary approach

do-good ideas

_____

_____

_____

SPEAKING 1

Communication Focus 1: Evaluating Arguments

Throughout the scientific process, input is evaluated. There are tools we can use to evaluate someone's argument or performance. Having a system for marking helps both the evaluator and the evaluated to understand what needs to be done prior to beginning the task and which areas need to be improved.

Columns in a rubric indicate if expectations have or haven't been met, while rows break down what is being evaluated. Brief descriptors clarify what must be done to achieve a certain score.

For example:

Case Study Report Rubric			
	Exceeds Expectations (2)	**Meets Expectations (1)**	**Doesn't Meet Expectations (0)**
Knowledge	skillful description of challenge	describes challenge	doesn't sufficiently describe challenge
Investigation	detailed portrayal of courses of action	lists courses of action	weak portrayal of courses of action
Presentation	fluent, vivid, engaging interactive presentation covers all points	presentation covers all points	unappealing; presentation lacks detail
Organization	tightly organized report, highly comprehensible	report is organized and comprehensible	organization unclear or lacking; difficult to follow

Another evaluation tool, a checklist, is easy to use. It organizes steps and procedures into manageable chunks. For example:

Today's seminar:

- ☐ The introduction helped participants prepare.
- ☐ Difficult vocabulary and ideas were explained in the introduction.
- ☐ The seminar team was well organized.
- ☐ The seminar team was well prepared.
- ☐ The seminar team used language skills accurately and effectively.
- ☐ The activities were interesting.
- ☐ The activities made participants think more deeply about the topic.
- ☐ Participants had abundant opportunity to participate.
- ☐ Downtime was minimized.
- ☐ The seminar team effectively summarized participant input.
- ☐ Participants enjoyed the seminar.
- ☐ Participants learned something.

Evaluators may use a **holistic approach** to evaluate something for its overall quality. With this approach, they consider all the elements, evaluating the performance as a whole, avoiding being overly concerned with separate elements.

Features of a holistic approach to evaluation:

1. It considers the general impression of the performance (speaking, writing, action).
2. It considers the overall quality of the performance.
3. It may involve the use of a team of evaluators (double, triple, or quadruple scoring).

4. It is based on pre-determined criteria, usually by a group.

5. It doesn't break down performance by separate skills, which might miss unexpected positive performance.

👥 SPEAKING ACTIVITY 1

Work with your partner to add to the list below of questions you may ask to evaluate a website. Use your questions to help you complete a website evaluation rubric.

Who wrote the information on the website? Is the website's author qualified?

What is the purpose of the website?

Is the information reliable?

Is the website easy to read and pleasing to the eye?

_____

_____

_____

Website Evaluation Rubric			
	Exceeds Expectations	**Meets Expectations**	**Doesn't Meet Expectations**
Source/author	qualified, accessible	connected to field, some contact info	no qualifications, no contact info
Purpose	clear, evident, to the point	some ideas clear; organization shaky	ideas unclear; pointless
Reliability	fact-based, sourced, cited	some unsupported points	opinion-based, unsourced
Optics (how it looks; its appearance)	attractive, appealing	typical, doesn't stand out	dull, messy, hard to read

👥 SPEAKING ACTIVITY 2

Work with your partner and brainstorm to add to the list of questions you would ask to evaluate a worker's performance. Then use your questions to help you create a worker's performance evaluation rubric. (This could be for any kind of worker, for example, for a server, a bus driver—anyone you come into regular contact with.)

1. Did the worker meet the expectations in performing the job functions?

2. Was the worker's behaviour helpful and well mannered?

3. Did the worker respond to your needs?
4. Did the worker enhance the effectiveness or image of the business?

_____ ?

_____ ?

_____ ?

Based on the questions you have asked, list the criteria in the left column, and your feedback in the other columns.

Worker Performance Evaluation Rubric			
	Exceeds Expectations	**Meets Expectations**	**Doesn't Meet Expectations**
Job completion			
Helpfulness			
Responsiveness			
Business image enhanced			

SPEAKING ACTIVITY 3

Work with your group to build a list of questions you would ask to evaluate a speech. Use your questions to help you create a speech evaluation rubric.

Q1. _____

Q2. _____

Q3. _____

Q4. _____

Speech Evaluation Rubric			
	Exceeds Expectations	**Meets Expectations**	**Doesn't Meet Expectations**
Grammatical accuracy			
Main point preview			

👥 SPEAKING ACTIVITY 4

With your partner, brainstorm services that you have paid for recently. Work with your partner to create **checklists** for what you expected from these services.

Example:

Car Inspection Checklist		
Service	Done	Not Done
Checked oil, fluids	✓	
Inspected brakes	✓	
Checked tire pressure	✓	
Checked lights		✓
Lubricated locks	✓	

_____Checklist		
Service	Done	Not Done

_____Checklist		
Service	Done	Not Done

👥 SPEAKING ACTIVITY 5

Talk with your partner about a movie you watched recently. Give it a rating out of 10 and explain why you scored it this way. Discuss with your partner what criteria you used to reach that score.

👥 SPEAKING ACTIVITY 6

Olympic judges give numerical scores to evaluate athletes' performance. Discuss with your group how you think they make these determinations. Choose an Olympic event that is judged and list some of the features the judges look for in this event. Then, discuss with your group what evaluation tools you think they may use, for example, checklists, rubrics, holistic scores, a combination of these, or something else.

Grammar Note: Using Emphatic Structures

When we want to reinforce a point or contradict another speaker's point, we can use one of the following emphatic structures. They are useful in conversation, discussions, and debates.

Auxiliary verbs	do/does/did, will	I'm not upset; I **did** pass the test after all.
Adverbs	actually, really, seldom, literally, at all	None of the questions were what I studied for **at all**. I **actually** remembered the whole book for the test.
Fixed expressions	What I think is . . . What they are doing is . . . That's what you think/say.	**What I think is** that the test should've been online. **What she is saying is** that it will succeed.

SPEAKING ACTIVITY 7

Rewrite the sentences below so that they begin with the emphatic structures provided. When you've finished, practise saying the sentences out loud to your partner. Compare your answers with those of other classmates.

1. The main character carried out most of the investigation. (actually)

   Actually, the main character carried out most of the investigation.

2. When leptons interact with protons they mediate weak interactions. (I do believe that)

   _____

3. Professor Thomson rarely posts lab assignments. (rarely does)

   _____

4. You will seldom see fireflies away from wetlands. (seldom will)

   _____

5. I have never seen behaviour like that. (never have)

   _____

SPEAKING ACTIVITY 8

Write responses to the questions below using the suggested emphatic structures. When you've finished, practise saying the sentences out loud with focus on the emphatic structure.

Example:

Person A: He doesn't help us very much with the answers, does he? (in fact, does)

Person B: In fact, he does help us with the answers.

A: You don't want this book, do you? (actually, do)

B: _____

A: I don't believe Susan brings her laptop to class every day, does she? (actually, does)

B: _____

A: Did Professor Williams post any of the assignments? (definitely, did)

B: _____

A: Can we finish this assignment on time? (surely, will)

B: _____

A: Did Rami do all of the work? (literally, did)

B: _____

LISTENING 2

Before You Listen

👥 PRE-LISTENING ACTIVITY 1

Discuss with your partner what jobs you have done and whether you were paid fairly or were underpaid. Discuss what fair pay is. What is minimum wage in your hometown, or where you live now? Is it fair? Why or why not?

👥 PRE-LISTENING ACTIVITY 2

Read the story "Interns in Canada," then discuss the questions that follow with your group.

Interns in Canada

Although anyone who works in Canada is covered by an Employment Standards Act, companies are not obliged to offer interns the protection the act offers if they are registered as students at a Canadian secondary or post-secondary institution. Similarly, students contracted as unpaid interns are not covered by an Occupational Health and Safety Act.

Judge Rules That Movie Studio Should Have Been Paying Interns

There are approximately one million undergraduate interns (students on work placement, co-op or internships) in the USA—approximately half are unpaid.

In 2010, two unpaid interns worked on the movie Black Swan gaining valuable experience in the movie industry. They worked just like the paid employees did, but for no money. One of them, Eric Glatt, ran errands for the director, taking lunch orders, taking out the trash, and assembling furniture. Glatt felt that he was being taken advantage of, and ended up suing Fox Searchlight for breaking minimum wage laws. The company argued that interns got resumé enhancement and gained an education about the inner workings of a production office.

In June, 2013 a New York judge determined that the movie set was not an educational environment and the studio benefited from the interns' work as regular employees.

(Source: Steven Greenhouse, *New York Times*, 11 June 2013.)

Follow-up to the Eric Glatt case:

- In November 2013 Fox Searchlight won the right to appeal the New York judge's decision.
- There is no formal method of counting or measuring the number of unpaid interns in Canada.

Questions: Would you work for no money? What reasons could there be to do so? Discuss with your group under what conditions you would work without pay, and what you could gain from doing this.

UPFRONT VOCABULARY

internship	a period of time during which a student or new graduate gets practical experience in a job*
minimum wage	the lowest amount of money that an employer is allowed to pay by law*
plaintiff	a person who makes a formal complaint against sb in court*
compensation	sth, especially money, that sb gives you because they have hurt you, or damaged sth that you own; payment for a service you have provided*
violate	to break a law, an agreement, etc.
unconscionable	so bad, immoral, etc. that it makes you feel ashamed*
stunt	sth that is done in order to attract people's attention*

*Definition courtesy of *Oxford Advanced Learner's Dictionary.*

 PRE-LISTENING VOCABULARY

Look at the 13 language chunks from the listening in the chart on the next page. Work with a partner and a dictionary to find collocations.

Example:

Language chunk	hands-on learning
Collocations	hands-on <u>approach</u>
	hands-on <u>experience</u>
	<u>independent</u> learning
	<u>active</u> learning

emulate a model	media conglomerate	common practice
emulate _____	media _____	common _____
emulate _____	media _____	common _____
_____ a model	_____ conglomerate	_____ practice
_____ a model	_____ conglomerate	_____ practice
formal method	raise money	mutual benefit
formal _____	raise _____	mutual _____
formal _____	raise _____	mutual _____
_____ method	_____ money	_____ benefit
_____ method	_____ money	_____ benefit
file a lawsuit	establish a reputation	build a portfolio
file a _____	establish _____	build a _____
file a _____	establish _____	build a _____
_____ a lawsuit	_____ a reputation	_____ a portfolio
_____ a lawsuit	_____ a reputation	_____ a portfolio
tack on a question	track the number of	present an opportunity
tack on _____	track _____	present _____
tack on _____	track _____	present _____
_____ a question	_____ the number of	_____ an opportunity
_____ a question	_____ the number of	_____ an opportunity

Check your answers with the rest of the class. When you've finished, practise using them in sentences.

Note-Taking

Track 82

Listening STRATEGY
A listener who is expected to provide a report must avoid taking sides or projecting biases while listening. It is important to wait until a point or argument has been made fully before beginning to formulate an opinion.

Unpaid internships are common practice in many fields and not paying an intern isn't necessarily illegal, but it can be, depending on the province and the circumstances. Eric Glatt is an intern who successfully sued his employer for non-payment of wages (see Pre-listening Activity 2 above). Maegan Smulders is the Canadian "super-intern" who completed 10 internships in 112 days.

Listen to the debate "Interns: To Pay or Not to Pay" for the first time. Take notes by dividing your page into two separate sections for the points Eric Glatt and Maegan Smulders make.

Eric   Maegan

Pple's labour should be valued by . . .   _____

_____   _____

_____   _____

Listening for the Main Ideas

Listen to the debate again, and use your notes to help you answer the questions.

 Track 83

1. What is Eric's position?
2. What is Maegan's position?
3. Eric calls Maegan's experience a stunt. Do you think it was?
4. Does the host take sides? If you believe so, give examples to support your point.
5. Who do you think "won" the debate, Eric or Maegan? Use examples to support your argument.

Listening Comprehension

Listen to the debate again and answer the questions. Answer "true" (T), "false" (F), or "not clear from the listening" (NC).

 **Track 84**

1. Eric won a court ruling against the use of interns in a Hollywood movie. ____
2. It is legal to hire interns in Canada without paying them. ____
3. Canada has a specific method for tracking the number of interns across the country. ____
4. Maegan did 10 internships in 112 days. ____
5. Doing an internship is a choice. ____
6. Some companies don't hire interns because they don't have the budget for it. ____
7. Maegan got sponsorships from all the companies she worked at. ____
8. Eric thinks Maegan's approach to negotiate for money after an internship is a good model. ____

Personalizing

Job descriptions include words and phrases like *enthusiastic*, *flexible*, *good at taking direction*, and *works independently*. Choose a department at your school that you and your partner would like to work in. Then, prepare and practise an oral job description (for example, a 30-second ad) using this kind of language.

Vocabulary and Language Chunks

Work with your partner to match the expressions in the first column with their definitions in the second. When you've finished checking the correct answers, practise making sentences with the language chunks.

Expressions	Meanings
1. a pool of	____ give automatic approval
2. to make the playing field equal	____ cause a widespread feeling of surprise
3. for the long haul	____ a small family business
4. any way, shape, or form	____ act in a very different way; to alter one's own opinion
5. to send a shockwave	____ a supply of available goods, vehicles, or people
6. to change one's tune	____ to create a fair, impartial starting point
7. a mom and pop store	____ for an extended time
8. to rubber stamp sth (v.)	____ in any possible way or conditions

SPEAKING 2

Communication Focus 2: Debating—Presenting Arguments

Debates encourage students to learn how to think, as opposed to learning what to think. Debates emphasize critical thinking and effective communication. They bring structure to the interaction between two sides, allowing them to express their points of view about a resolution (debate topic) in an organized manner. Successful debaters share characteristics such as:

- confident, persuasive style of **expression**
- varied **tone** with strategic stress placement and clear **pronunciation**
- appropriate, confident **body language**
- appropriate **vocabulary** choices
- organized, effective, supported arguments

Overview of the Debate Process

1. The resolution is introduced and each speaker is allotted a time limit.
2. Debaters for the topic (the resolution) and against the resolution present constructive speeches.
3. Debaters present opposing follow-up (or counter-) arguments.
4. Debaters field questions from the audience.

👥 SPEAKING ACTIVITY 9

Divide into groups. Each group needs a number of index cards matching the number of members in the group. Mark an X on one card. Hand out the cards face down (hiding the X). Participants prepare statements about something unusual they have actually done, but the participant who has the X card creates statements based on an entirely false experience. Then, participants listen to each other's statements, ask questions, and eventually guess which is the false story. Speakers should try hard to be convincing and use the characteristics described in Communication Focus 2.

Speaking STRATEGY 💬

Prepare or familiarize yourself with specific vocabulary related to your topic prior to participating in a lecture, seminar, conversation, or discussion.

👥 SPEAKING ACTIVITY 10

"Weighing the pros and cons" means considering the advantages and disadvantages (the reasons for and the reasons against) an argument or course of action. In the following activity, take turns with a partner to express your position for each resolution clearly and confidently. Include a reason with each statement.

Example:

Resolution: **People should live in the country rather than in the city.**

Position: **I agree/disagree with the statement that people should live in the country.**

Reason: (pro/for) **It is healthier.**

Reason: (con/against) **Medical support is farther away.**

Resolution: International students caught working without visas should be immediately deported.

Position: _____

Reason: _____

Resolution: Junk food should be banned from schools.

Position: _____

Reason: _____

Resolution: Beauty contests should be banned.

Position: _____

Reason: _____

Resolution: Parental love is stronger than romantic love.

Position: _____

Reason: _____

ÅÅ SPEAKING ACTIVITY 11

Work with your partner and brainstorm further arguments to support the resolutions.

Resolution 1: People should live in the country instead of the city.

Argument 1. **Country life is healthier than city life.**

Argument 2. _____

Argument 3. _____

Argument 4. _____

Argument 5. _____

Resolution 2: Outside classroom (extracurricular) learning is more beneficial than in-class learning.

Argument 1. **My father taught me to drive—that was important.**

Argument 2. _____

Argument 3. _____

Argument 4. _____

Argument 5. _____

Resolution 3: Wild animals should not be kept in captivity.

Argument 1. **Zoos are prisons.**

Argument 2. _____

Argument 3. _____

Argument 4. _____

Argument 5. _____

ÅÅ SPEAKING ACTIVITY 12

With your partner, choose one of the following resolutions, then work together to build a brief supporting argument (three or four sentences) for it by using facts, examples, comparisons, quotes, or anecdotes.

Example:

> **Air pollution affects our daily activities.**
> a. **(fact) 5,900 deaths can be linked to air pollution every year.**
> b. **(comparison) If the air quality is at levels 1–3, the general population can enjoy regular outdoor activities, but if the air quality level is 7–10, people should reduce their outdoor activities.**
>
> (Source: Government of Canada, "The Air Quality Health Index: How Pollution Affects Your Health.")

1. International students caught working without visas should be immediately deported.

2. The customer is always right.

3. If your product can be produced in another country more cheaply, do it.

4. The purpose of a corporation is to earn profit for its investors.

Communication Focus 3: Debating—Presenting Counter-Arguments

A counter-argument is a response to an argument in a debate. Take notes while the other team is talking so that you can identify mistakes, contradictions, lack of evidence, flaws in logic, or assumptions.

Some helpful counter-argument language:

You say . . .	but such is not the case.	Actually, . . .
Your team argues . . .	There is a flaw in your logic.	In fact, . . .
_____ has stated . . .	You are missing an important detail.	
[person]	but as we have already made clear, . . .	
	On the contrary . . .	
	It's a moot point.	

👥 SPEAKING ACTIVITY 13

Groups can practise this warm-up activity by sitting in a circle and taking turns disagreeing on a statement related to a topic.

Example:

> **Topic: Interns**
>
> Student 1: Interns don't need to be paid, they get good on-the-job training.
>
> Student 2: I disagree entirely. They work as hard as the paid employees.
>
> Student 3: You say they don't need to be paid, but not paying them is illegal.

After each student has spoken, change topics. Student 2 will start. Go until each group member has had a turn starting.

Topics:

- international students' tuition
- using cell phones in class
- using one's first language in an ESL class
- minimum wage (from an employer's perspective)
- minimum wage (from an employee's perspective)

ᴊᴊ SPEAKING ACTIVITY 14

Take turns with your partner finding weaknesses in the following claims, and then practise countering them.

Example:

> **Claim:** A lot of Canadians would rather spend winter holidays in Florida than in Canada.
>
> **Counter-argument:** The phrases "A lot of Canadians," and "would rather spend" are vague. Actually, only 17 percent of Canadians per year travel to the southern states for winter holidays.

1. In the fourth quarter of the year profits increased $360,000; that's $90,000 per quarter.

2. A school year is too short (180 school days). If the school year were longer, more kids would succeed.

3. There have been fewer terrorist attacks since 2001, so anti-terror programs are working.

4. Jean Chrétien refused to send Canadian troops to fight in Iraq; evidently, he hates Canada.

5. Xander College is the number-one college in the province; it says so in their brochures.

6. According to the National Association of Teachers, junk food should be banned from schools.

Grammar Note: Using Noun Clauses as Embedded Questions

We can use a noun clause to provide a fuller explanation of the subject or object of a sentence.

> Subject: The <u>car</u> (<u>that</u>) <u>I bought</u>   Object: I read <u>what you wrote</u>.
> broke down.

When a noun clause is an embedded question it keeps its statement order (subject–verb–object). Embedded questions can begin with a question word such as *if, whether,* or *that*:

She has no idea <u>who paid the bill</u>.	I don't know <u>what time it is</u>.
Please tell me <u>where you live</u>.	I wonder <u>when he finishes work</u>.
I can't imagine <u>why I ate it</u>.	I told them <u>how you got here</u>.
I can't remember <u>if I saw it</u>.	Advise me <u>whether I should buy it (or not)</u>.
I hope <u>that they will attend the party</u>.	I heard him say <u>that pies are square</u>.

👥 SPEAKING ACTIVITY 15

Change the direct questions below to sentences with embedded questions. Then, work with your partner to complete and practise the dialogue between a business teacher and a student.

Who is the CEO of Loblaw Company?	Please teach <u>me who the CEO of Loblaw Company is.</u>
What does a CEO do?	Please help me understand _____
Where does Galen Weston work?	Could you tell me _____
When will the next quarter end?	Can you inform me _____
Why is Loblaw Company successful?	Please explain _____
How did Mr. Weston become CEO?	Could you explain to me _____

Dialogue:

Student: Good morning, Ms. Ostrom.

Teacher: Good morning, Seth.

Student: Ms. Ostrom, I'm studying Canadian business. Could you tell me who Galen Weston is?

Teacher: Sure, Seth, he is the one who manages Loblaws, a Canadian supermarket chain.

_____

_____

_____

_____

_____

👥 SPEAKING ACTIVITY 16

Build and practise a dialogue between a senior student and a first-year student who needs help adjusting to campus life. Use phrases (such as those listed in the chart on the next page) in sentences with noun clauses.

Example: need to know

　　Excuse me; I <u>need to know</u> <u>who it is that takes care of registration.</u>
　　　　　　　　[phrase]　　　　　　　　　　　[noun clause]

Phrases			
First-year student		**Senior student**	
would like to know	wonder	I know that . . .	Let me show you how to . . .
don't know	can't remember	I think that . . .	
need to know	want to find out	Room A14 is the place where . . .	

PRONUNCIATION

Pronunciation Focus: Using Common Intonation Patterns—Part 2

 **Track 85**

In the following thought groups, the primary stress is <u>underlined</u>. Note how intonation rises or falls following the primary stress.

1. Taking turns in conversation:	(a) rising (unfinished) I finished the <u>first</u> part, <u>but</u> . . . (b) falling (finished) On the midterm I got a <u>ninety</u>.
2. a. Tag questions: rising (asking)	You have pre<u>pared</u> for this, haven't <u>you</u>?
b. Tag questions: falling (commentary)	You're from <u>Halifax</u>, <u>aren't</u> you?
3. Questions to check or confirm: rise at end	Ex<u>cuse</u> me, do you have a minute to <u>spare</u>? <u>Sorry</u>, what time is the next <u>bus</u>?
4. Enthusiasm: rise and extended or sharp fall on focus word	Tomorrow's test is <u>cancelled</u>! That's <u>greeaaat</u> neeeeeeeewwws!
5. Surprise: rising	That was <u>you</u>? <u>Really</u>?
6. Confusion: rising	<u>What</u> did the prof want me to do?
7. Anger: punctuated stress	<u>That's</u> the <u>second</u> <u>time</u> you've <u>done</u> that!
8. Sarcasm: flat	<u>Nice</u> <u>shirt</u>.

PRONUNCIATION ACTIVITY 1

 **Track 86**

Work with a partner. Consider the following common expressions. Listen to the different ways they are pronounced and discuss how pronouncing them differently changes them.

1. Yes.
2. Thank you.
3. Welcome.

PRONUNCIATION ACTIVITY 2

 **Track 87**

With your partner, recall the discussions you had in Pronunciation Activity 1. Listen carefully, and repeat the word *yes* the same way it is said each time.

1. Flat intonation (of *yes*) means you are not really interested in the question or request.

   A: Are you enjoying the lecture?　　B: Yes.

2. Falling intonation of *yes* means that you agree with what is being said or asked.

   A: Is there another lecture tomorrow?　B: Yes.

3. Rising intonation of *yes* means you are asking for clarification.

   A: The lecture's at 2:00 PM.　　B: Yes? (Really?)

4. If the intonation of *yes* rises then stretches and falls, it means you are not sure about what was said.

   A: And then everyone will sign up.　　B: Ye-es. (I don't follow/I don't understand.)

PRONUNCIATION ACTIVITY 3

 **Track 88**

Listen to the various ways the following sentence is said. When the audio has finished, take turns with your partner saying the sentence, placing stress on a different word each time. When you are finished discuss the different meanings.

He didn't say Susan had to attend the rally.

He **didn't** say Susan had to attend the rally.

He didn't **say** Susan had to attend the rally.

He didn't say **Su**san had to attend the rally.

He didn't say Susan **had** to attend the rally.

He didn't say Susan had to **attend** the rally.

He didn't say Susan had to attend the **ral**ly.

PRONUNCIATION ACTIVITY 4

Track 89

In English the various intonation patterns each have a specific meaning. To review this important feature, listen to and identify the intonation patterns in the following sentences. What is the speaker doing? Choose the correct intention beside the sentence and underline it.

1. Stating a fact or asking a question?

a.	They send teams of three to five students	stating a fact	asking a question
b.	They won the case	stating a fact	asking a question
c.	Maegan Smulders took 12 intern jobs	stating a fact	asking a question

2. Commenting or checking?

a.	They send teams of three to five students.	commenting	checking
b.	They won the case.	commenting	checking
c.	Maegan Smulders took 12 intern jobs.	commenting	checking

3. Giving an open list or giving a closed list?

a.	The field team set up nurseries in Ghana, Nigeria, Burkina Faso.	giving an open list	giving a closed list
b.	They started up nurseries, groceries, farms.	giving an open list	giving a closed list
c.	Maegan was offered jobs in Las Vegas, Toronto, and Montreal.	giving an open list	giving a closed list

PRONUNCIATION ACTIVITY 5

Track 90

Listen to and identify the intonation patterns in the following as unfinished or finished. Underline the correct type. Share your answers with a partner.

1.	I believe that no internship should be unpaid	finished	unfinished
2.	Unpaid internships are necessary	finished	unfinished
3.	I don't believe an education is enough for young people these days	finished	unfinished
4.	I wouldn't say they become less valuable	finished	unfinished
5.	You want to do better in the long haul	finished	unfinished

PRONUNCIATION ACTIVITY 6

Listen to the following tag questions and identify them as to type: **commentary** or **question**. If it's a question, respond appropriately. Note that the end punctuation has been left out.

 **Track 91**

Example:

| **They've made a decision, haven't they** | (This is a commentary; intonation is falling; no response is needed.) |

Example:

| **You started developing a program that focuses on small businesses, didn't you** | (This is a question; intonation is rising; response is necessary.) |

Here's one possible response: **Yes we did.**

1. If all interns had to be paid, companies would stop hiring them, wouldn't they _____

2. Somebody has to do the things that interns are doing, don't they

   _____

3. They add value, create jobs, and create incomes, don't they

   _____

4. We try to get to businesses along that supply chain, don't we

   _____

5. We should go directly to these entrepreneurs, shouldn't we

   _____

PRONUNCIATION ACTIVITY 7

Sometimes the same group of words can be expressed in differing ways to show different emotions. For example, the sentence "Deldar got the job" can express any one of these emotions:

Track 92

a. enthusiasm   b. confusion   c. anger   or   d. sarcasm

Listen carefully to each sentence and indicate which emotion is being expressed. Share your answers with your partner.

1. Deldar got the job.   _____
2. Deldar got the job.   _____
3. Deldar got the job.   _____
4. Deldar got the job.   _____

 **Track 93**

 PRONUNCIATION ACTIVITY 8

Listen to the sentences and identify how the speaker infuses emotion into each sentence. Confirm your answers with a partner.

Example:

> You will be on time for class tomorrow, won't you.

> How does the speaker express mistrust?

> The speaker stretches *will* and the tag intonation is flat.

Do you think that those experiences become less valuable when you're paid for them?

1. How does the speaker express surprise?

    _____

You said that the geraniums are to be planted over here.

2. How does the speaker express confusion?

    _____

He worked for three months. He needs to be paid.

3. How does the speaker express anger?

    _____

PRONUNCIATION ACTIVITY 9

Work with a partner to find famous movie quotes on the Internet. Listen carefully and challenge each other to mimic the emotions expressed and intonation/stress techniques used. Here are some names to help you get started, but you may also have some quotes or movie stars of your own to reference.

Mae West (in *I'm No Angel*, 1933):

"When I'm good, I'm very good, but when I'm bad, I'm better."

Groucho Marx:

"I've had a very perfectly wonderful evening, but this wasn't it."

Arnold Schwarzenegger (in *The Terminator*, 1984)

"I'll be back."

Clark Gable (in *Gone with the Wind*, 1939)

"Frankly my dear, I don't give a damn."

ññ PRONUNCIATION ACTIVITY 10

Read the dialogue below with your partner. Use your own interpretation of the mood the characters might feel. Then make your own similar, original dialogue.

The Overnight Train

Conductor: Tickets!

Passenger: Grmph. *[sleeping]* Yes?

Conductor: Please wake up sir, I need to see your ticket.

Passenger: Sure. I've got it, uhm, right, uhm here, I think. *[continues searching]*

Conductor: Ticket please.

Passenger: Yes, yes. Here you go.

Conductor: *[inspecting ticket]* Uhm sir, I'm sorry, this ticket is not valid.

Passenger: What are you talking about? I bought it this afternoon.

Conductor: Sir, it's two weeks old. It's not even for this line.

Passenger: There must be a mistake.

Conductor: No mistake. I'm sorry, but I have to ask you to get off the train at the next stop.

Passenger: In the middle of the night? In the middle of nowhere? You're kicking me off the train 'cause your agent sold me the wrong ticket?

Conductor: No sir. I'm asking you to get off the train because your snoring is driving everyone crazy.

COMMUNICATING IN THE REAL WORLD

In an academic context, debates are an essential way to consider the various aspects of a given topic. A debate requires a complex use of language and will allow you to practise a variety of language functions learned in this textbook including **being concise** (Chapter 1), **describing problems** (Chapter 1), **using discourse markers** (Chapter 3), **paraphrasing** (Chapter 2), **summarizing** (Chapter 6), and **synthesizing information** (Chapter 6), along with the skills you have learned in this chapter:

- expressing a position
- supporting an argument
- evaluating what people do and say
- reflecting about what people have said
- responding to an argument; using emphatic structures
- using intonation patterns with intent

You will now put all these skills to use in a real debate. The suggestions and information on the next page will help you get organized and hold your debate.

Debate

Organize yourselves into two teams of five and decide on a topic for your debate. One team will be in favour of the statement chosen, taking the "Pro" position; the other team will oppose the statement, taking the "Con" position. (This structure can be varied to work with any number of participants.)

(Team A) "Pro"	(Team B) "Con"
A1	B1
A2	B2
A3	B3
A4	B4
A5	B5

Sample topics:

Canadians should be more involved supporting small businesses in developing economies.

A co-op, internship, or field trip should be a program requirement for every graduate.

Eating meat is immoral.

Students need to have their smartphones in class.

Cohabitation is a replacement for marriage.

Your own topic: _____

Debate Procedure	
1.	Moderator introduces the resolution.
2.	Speaker A1 states the pro team's first argument.
3.	Speaker B1 states the con team's first argument.
4.	Speaker B2 counters Speaker A1's argument.
5.	Speaker A2 counters Speaker B1's argument.
6.	Speaker A3 states the pro team's second argument.
7.	Speaker B3 states the con team's second argument.
8.	Speaker B4 counters Speaker A3's argument.
9.	Speaker A4 counters Speaker B3's argument.
10.	Speaker A5 summarizes team A's argument.
11.	Speaker B5 summarizes team B's argument.
12.	Moderator manages questions and commentary from audience.

SELF-EVALUATION

Think about your work in this chapter. For each row in the chart sections **Grammar and Language Functions**, **Pronunciation**, **Learning Strategies**, and **Note-Taking**, give yourself a score based on the rating scale below and write a comment in the Notes section.

Show the chart to your teacher. Talk about what you need to do to make your English better.

Rating Scale

1	2	3	4	5

Needs improvement. ←——————————————→ *Great!*

	Score	Notes
Grammar and Language Functions		
evaluating arguments		
using emphatic structures		
debating (presenting arguments)		
debating (presenting counter-arguments)		
using noun clauses as embedded questions		
Pronunciation		
using common intonation patterns—Part 2		
Learning Strategies		
Speaking		
familiarizing myself with contextual vocabulary		
Listening		
asking reflective questions		
avoiding bias		
Note-Taking		
pausing and reflecting		
organizing by speaker		

Vocabulary and Language Chunks

Look at this list of new vocabulary and language chunks you learned in this chapter. Give yourself a score based on the rating scale and write a comment.

engage s/o	abolish	Arab Spring	file a lawsuit
entrepreneur	slavery	multi-disciplinary	flag a concern
determinism	bondage	approach	build a portfolio
emerging	internship	do-good ideas	tack on a question
NGO	minimum wage	case study	track the number of
nutrition	plaintiff	roll up (one's) sleeves	present an opportunity
integrated	compensation	rapid change	emulate a model
innovative	violate	flagship program	establish a reputation
evaluate	unconscionable	moral imperative	a pool of
phenomenal	stunt	hands-on learning	make the playing field
heartland		media conglomerate	equal
sustainable		common practice	for the long haul
instability		formal method	any way, shape, or form
rapidity		raise money	send a shockwave
		mutual benefit	change one's tune
			a mom and pop store
			to rubber stamp sth

	Score	Notes
understanding new vocabulary and language chunks		
using new lexical items freely and confidently		

My plan for practising is _____

_____

_____

_____

CHAPTER 8

Transitioning to Professional Life

Preparing for a job interview

Arguing persuasively

Negotiating

THINKING AND TALKING

Applying for a position in a company can be a stressful experience, especially if you don't know what to expect. From searching for and finding the right job to crafting a resumé and a cover letter and participating in a job interview, the transition from graduating to a career involves careful consideration and planning.

Get together with a few of your classmates and discuss the following questions. Have you ever held a job? What has your job application experience been? What are some strategies you know that would give an edge (advantage) to a job applicant?

LISTENING 1

Before You Listen

PRE-LISTENING ACTIVITY 1

Canadian resumés may be different than resumés in the country where you are from; customs for what content should be included and what content should be avoided may differ.

A. Work on your own and check all the items in the checklist below that you believe should be included on a Canadian resumé.

B. When you are finished, compare your answers with those of a small group of your classmates and discuss the reasons behind your choices.

- ☐ education, including what you are currently studying, even if you are not yet finished
- ☐ a picture of your face so the employer can make an immediate personal connection with you
- ☐ personal data including height, weight, and age
- ☐ your Twitter handle
- ☐ school and/or work awards
- ☐ a link to your Facebook page
- ☐ contact information, including your phone number and email address
- ☐ family information: number of children; whether you are expecting a child
- ☐ marital status: single, married, divorced
- ☐ a list of your hobbies
- ☐ certifications and licences
- ☐ work experience
- ☐ sports that you play
- ☐ other _____

👥👥👥 PRE-LISTENING ACTIVITY 2

Work in your same groups and brainstorm ideas that would make your resumé stand out effectively from resumés of other candidates—try to "think outside the box."

Examples:

> use high quality paper
>
> highlight the link between your skills and the job requirements

UPFRONT VOCABULARY

entrepreneur	a person who makes money by starting or running businesses*
milestone	a very important stage or event in the development of sth*
hackathon	(hack + marathon) a software creation event in which developers and computer programmers work together intensively on software projects
per se	by itself—used to show that you are referring to sth on its own, rather than in connection with other things*
freelancer	a person who sells his or her work piece by piece rather than working for one employer

*Definition courtesy of *Oxford Advanced Learner's Dictionary.*

👥👥 PRE-LISTENING VOCABULARY

Using a dictionary to help you, circle the word that is the best fit in each sentence. Then, show your answers to your partner and explain your choices. There may be more than one correct answer.

1. This topic is extremely (relevant/meaningful) to my study.
2. The new airport runway is rather (wide/broad).
3. Stu brought copies of his (CV/resumé/work history) to the job interview.
4. Heather's (profile/background) impressed the interviewers.
5. The answers to life's key questions are often (elusive/difficult/tricky).
6. Money markets, banks, and brokers are found in the financial (zone/sector/area).
7. The magazine has few staff so they use (freelance/outsourced) photographers.
8. When I crossed the border the immigration officer asked if I had anything to (declare/claim/state).
9. It is well known that Bill Gates (founded/discovered) Microsoft.

Note-Taking

 **Track 94**

When applying for a job, applicants traditionally use a one- or two-page document called a resumé. This document contains the job applicant's educational background, work experience, achievements, and awards that are pertinent to the potential job. A CV (*curriculum vitae*) is different from a resumé in that it is longer and contains much more career-oriented detail. CVs are commonly used by professors, researchers, lawyers, or senior executives who already have a distinguished career.

You will listen to the CBC interview "The New Resumé," with Christopher (Chris) Kennedy. He believes that traditional resumés are no longer relevant in today's job market that encourages hiring freelancers and project-based consultants. Chris is a founding partner of Status Chart, a very successful website which helps freelancers showcase their past and present accomplishments as well as their future endeavours.

Contrast similarities and differences in your notes by organizing the information in side-by-side columns. This helps you understand the differences. Listen to the interview for the first time and list what you hear about resumés and CVs in the column on the left. List details you hear about the Status Chart website in the column on the right.

Resumés/CVs	Status Chart

Listening for the Main Ideas

 **Track 95**

Listen to the interview "The New Resumé" once again and add to the lists you made for the previous listening activity, then use your notes to help you answer the questions. When you are finished, compare your answers with those of a partner.

Listening STRATEGY

Because speakers don't always use clear language to list their examples, it is helpful while listening to itemize, in list form, the key information given.

1. According to Chris Kennedy, what is the main weakness of a resumé?

   _____

2. What is the main difference between the website Status Chart and a resumé?

   _____

3. According to the interviewer, how has public opinion changed about the idea of a job for life?

    _____

4. According to Chris, how is Status Chart honest?

    _____

5. Why does Chris feel that, in his case at least, a resumé was worthless?

    _____

Listening Comprehension

Listen to the interview "The New Resumé" once again and answer the questions by underlining the correct response. When you are finished, compare your answers with those of a partner.

 **Track 96**

1. How long would Chris's resumé be if it included everything he has done?
    a. 10 pages
    b. more than 10 pages
    c. endless

2. What kind of professionals is Status Chart aimed at?
    a. freelancers, designers, and developers
    b. professionals who pay attention to details
    c. the tech community

3. Status Chart best
    a. replaces a resumé entirely
    b. allows a resumé to stand out
    c. works with a resumé

4. According to the audio clip, what do some employers do?
    a. They use computer software to find key words instead of reading the resumés.
    b. They focus on the education aspect of resumés.
    c. They try to paint a clear picture of a candidate's education and work experience.

5. What feature of Status Chart is not referred to in the audio clip?
    a. Status Chart categorizes projects as "on hold," "completed," and "in progress."
    b. Status Chart keeps track of everything that its users are doing.
    c. Status Chart is more detailed than the broad brushstroke style of a resumé.

Personalizing

Brainstorm with your partner
to create an oral resumé.
Start by making a quick list of
one each of your educational
experiences, work experiences,
projects, skills, strengths, and
goals. When you've got your
lists ready, present them orally,
with some elaboration as
time permits.

Vocabulary and Language Chunks

Work with your partner to
match the words in the first
column with their definitions in the second. When you've finished,
practise making sentences with the target language chunks.

Language Chunks

1. paint an accurate picture

2. have a 9-to-5 job

3. paint with broad strokes
4. cheat the system

5. stay on top of things
6. have a sense of community

7. come to the realization
8. go above and beyond

9. avoid at all costs
10. do more damage than good

Definitions

____ succeed by following a
non-conventional procedure

____ be employed full-time

____ have an overall negative effect

____ describe in general terms
without focusing on details

_1_ describe clearly and fairly

____ do one's best not to experience
or come in contact with

____ be in control of situations

____ understand the value of
interpersonal relationships

____ learn or understand eventually

____ do more than is expected

SPEAKING 1

Communication Focus 1: Preparing for a Job Interview

Job interviews are stressful; however, with the right preparation
and understanding that most interviewers ask essentially the same
questions, you can be successful and start working in your dream career
right away.

Often, the first question you will be asked is about how you would describe yourself. It is important in your job interview preparation that you organize your ideas and answer according to your educational and job experience, not your personal life. Use these phrases to show your accomplishments:

I have learned . . .

I have developed . . .

I have created . . .

Next, you may be asked about your strengths. For this question, you should give specific examples of what you are good at. Use language that is active and shows specific examples of your successes.

Examples:

Passive	Active
. . . happened to me	I did . . .
I received	I successfully pursued . . .
I was given	I have achieved . . .
I was responsible for	I accomplished . . .

You will likely also be asked to describe a weaknesses or a difficult situation you have had to deal with. To answer this question successfully, you must be careful to be honest, but choose a weakness or situation that you can show in a positive way or show how you have successfully overcome it.

Examples:

Weakness	Positive Spin
slow at completing a task	You are careful to avoid mistakes.
not detail oriented	You can focus on the big picture.
afraid of public speaking	You have taken classes to practise.
weakness in English	You speak {other} language(s) as well as English.

👥 SPEAKING ACTIVITY 1

Choose five of the eight common interview questions that follow. Work with a partner and practise asking and answering them by using language in Communication Focus 1, talking about your strengths, and putting a positive spin on weaknesses.

1. How would you describe yourself?
2. What is your greatest strength?
3. What is your greatest weakness?
4. Why are you the best person for this job?
5. How would your past colleagues/employer describe you?

Speaking STRATEGY 💬

Promote yourself at a job interview by being honest, giving specific examples of your achievements, showing that you are proud of your achievements, and asking questions about the job that show you have done research about the company and you would like to learn more.

6. Tell us something about yourself that's not on your resumé.

7. Define teamwork.

8. How do you handle stress and pressure?

👥 SPEAKING ACTIVITY 2

Read the job posting and jot down five reasons why you would be a good candidate for this job. Then ask your partner for five reasons why he or she would be a good candidate for this job.

2-year fixed term Food Taster Position

Applications are invited for the position of Full-time Food Taster, Pay Band H, serving in the Food Products Division. The starting salary is $19.70/hr for a 35-hour week. Some flexible scheduling of hours, including evenings and weekends, is required.

Reporting to the Manager of Food Services, the Food Taster provides a full range of evaluation and critique services.

Required qualifications include:

- A three (3) year college diploma or a university degree in a related area of culinary studies, chef training, or biology
- Some experience in inter-office communication and working in a factory environment
- Proven communication, people management, problem solving, and time management skills
- Knowledge of Canada's food industry
- Preference will be given to those holding valid certification in food safety.

I would be a good candidate for the job because:

Reason 1. _____

Reason 2. _____

Reason 3. _____

Reason 4. _____

Reason 5. _____

👥 SPEAKING ACTIVITY 3

Providing references is necessary when applying for a job. To be a reference for someone else means that you vouch for (guarantee) that person's skills, abilities, and/or work ethic. In most cases, a reference is someone who has had a supervisory role, for example, a manager, boss, or teacher.

Using the information each of you have collected in Speaking Activity 2 and adding your own knowledge of your classmates, work in small groups to practise being a reference for each other. Each person should take a turn acting as a reference for another student in the group until everyone has had a turn to speak.

👥 SPEAKING ACTIVITY 4

Work on your own and think about four general facts about yourself (your hometown, your country, etc.) that you will share with your group. When everyone is ready, take turns telling your information in groups of four while remaining seated and comfortable.

Once everyone has had a turn, join two groups together. This time, stand up one at a time, taking turns presenting your information more formally to the larger group.

Share reflections with the larger group about how you felt while telling your information in a comfortable sitting position to a small group and how it felt different when you had to present to a larger group. Split back into the original groups and discuss what the effects were of the speakers' body language.

👥 SPEAKING ACTIVITY 5

Set up in groups of three. Read each of the following three job descriptions carefully and then role play job interviews, alternating roles for each posting.

Role A: Interviewer. Select questions from Speaking Activity 1, and add some of your own.

Role B: Interviewee. Prepare by anticipating some of the questions from Speaking Activity 1.

Role C: Observer. As the interview progresses, take notes, including your observations about your partners' usage of language skills and body language. After each interview is finished, share your observations with your group mates.

Interviews 2 and 3: Do the same for the other two mock job interviews, rotating parts so that each group member gets to play each role.

Job Posting 1

> **RL Real Estate** is looking for an entry-level social media expert to help post, tag, tweet, Instagram, brainstorm, and support a variety of marketing initiatives.
>
> This is a great opportunity for someone to take charge of a media strategy to promote client service and communication.
>
> You will work autonomously on creative tasks and develop your media skills.
>
> The successful applicant will have excellent written and verbal communication skills and is interested in expanding on these skills.
>
> Proven work experience with social media is an asset.

Job Posting 2

> ### Rogtech Call Centre is Expanding!
> ### We are now accepting applications.
>
> We offer:
> - extensive training
> - rapid career advancement
> - competitive compensation, bonuses, and incentives
>
> We are looking for people:
> - with a positive attitude
> - who have the desire to succeed
> - who have a great work ethic and competitive spirit
>
> Requirements:
> - ability to work in a team environment and with customers
> - can contribute to a professional, positive work environment

Job Posting 3

> ### STEINGART
>
> **Steingart Equipment** is one of Ontario's leading construction machinery repair companies. The successful applicant will work with a senior technician and the service coordinator to assist in parts inventory management and equipment maintenance. General mechanical aptitude, a willingness to learn, and excellent verbal communication skills are essential for this exciting position.

Communication Focus 2: Arguing Persuasively

Speakers may need to change listeners' perceptions, their way of thinking about an issue, or their behaviour. Techniques that support persuasive speaking include:

- making explicit claims about the effectiveness or benefits of what you are suggesting: **saves, improves, enhances**
- using intensifiers: **the best, the highest, the safest, the most useful . . .**
- asking rhetorical questions: **Do you want to succeed? Do you want to know the answers?**
- using analogy: **this means . . ., this is said when . . ., this implies . . .**

- using sensory language: descriptive words about what is
  - seen: **hazy, glistening, . . .**
  - felt: **lukewarm, searing, . . .**
  - heard: **rustling, shrill, . . .**
  - smelled: **pungent, fishy, . . .**
  - tasted: **vinegary, spicy, . . .**
- using inclusive language: **as you know . . ., everyone agrees . . ., wouldn't you agree . . .**
- citing experiences: **in the past . . . , imagine your . . .**
- using testimonials (comments and feedback from customers, clients, employers): **according to . . ., [someone] reported . . .**
- repeating key language or points: **as you heard me say earlier . . ., as you may recall . . .**
- anticipating and handling objections: **on the contrary . . ., you may ask yourself . . .**

Grammar Note: Applying the Passive Voice

To show readers or listeners that we are stating something factual and unbiased, we can use the passive voice to gain their trust. Passive voice can be applied to portray an unbiased, factual account. The passive voice is formed by shifting the focus of the sentence from the subject to the object using

- *to be* as the helping verb to indicate tense, and
- the main verb in its past participle form

Note how the usage of the passive voice in these example sentences puts the focus on what is actually being talked about:

> It <u>is well known</u> that overuse of certain prescription drugs is causing a significant social problem.
>
> The benefits of antibiotics <u>have been studied</u> for years.
>
> The practical uses <u>were demonstrated</u> quite effectively by Dr. Yeo in his early experiments.
>
> The results of the research <u>will be published</u> later this year.

👥 SPEAKING ACTIVITY 6

Presenting information factually supports a persuasive argument. With your partner, practise using the expressions below to make factual statements.

Stating Facts
It's a well-known fact that . . .
It has been demonstrated/proven that . . .
It has been reported/stated that . . .
It is understood that . . .
It is (commonly) accepted as true that . . .

👥 SPEAKING ACTIVITY 7

Work in groups of three. Two students each choose a favourite travel destination and take turns attempting to convince the third student to travel there on his or her next holiday. The third student then chooses the more persuasive argument of the two and explains why it was successful. Then change roles and practise persuading the others where to go for dinner or what program to study.

Turkey

Thailand

Switzerland

France

Speaking STRATEGY 💬

The word that appears most consistently in successful persuasive speeches and marketing is *you*. This is a reminder that the focus in persuasive communication should be on the listener, not the speaker.

👥 SPEAKING ACTIVITY 8

Choose one of the following situations and work with a partner to build a dialogue. Use at least three different persuasive techniques from Communication Focus 2 to make your arguments more convincing.

(Situation 1: you and parent) You are unmarried. Explain why you should be allowed to move in with your significant other.

(Situation 2: you and campus food services manager) Explain why the cafeteria should sell different kinds of food.

(Situation 3: you and parking enforcement officer) Explain why you shouldn't have to pay a parking ticket.

👥 SPEAKING ACTIVITY 9

Prepare a persuasive argument in order to convince: (1) a friend; (2) your parents; (3) a classmate to join you on a trip to an out-of-town job fair. Take turns with your partner switching roles (persuader/persuadee).

👥 SPEAKING ACTIVITY 10

Your city has had a windfall! The provincial government has found that a local casino should have been paying taxes over the last five years, and has ordered the casino to pay those back taxes ($8 million) to your city immediately.

Job Fair

Divide the class into seven groups. Each group will attempt to persuade the rest of the other groups for a share of the money. Make a strong case for your group by using persuasive techniques from this chapter.

- Group A supports upgrading the gym at your college/university: $3.5 million
- Group B supports improving road and streetlight conditions: $4 million

- Group C supports upgrades to municipal transit for new buses and trains: $3.5 million
- Group D supports adding a new wing to the local hospital and hiring four nurses: $4.5 million
- Group E supports upgrading the local sports complex: $4.5 million
- Group F supports expanding the Municipal Arts Centre: $4 million
- Group G (can decide on their own how much and for what purpose)

SPEAKING ACTIVITY 11

Combine concepts from Communication Focus 1 and Communication Focus 2 to create a strong persuasive argument for why you are the best person for:

1. class president
2. valedictorian
3. international student association president
4. class social activities organizer
5. new hire at Company X

LISTENING 2

Before You Listen

PRE-LISTENING ACTIVITY 1

Have you or someone you know ever been hacked? Work with a partner and imagine that someone you don't know is trying to learn as much about you as possible. Discuss how they would go about it online. How much and what kind of information would they be able to find out about you?

PRE-LISTENING ACTIVITY 2

Work in small groups to discuss the idea of privacy in today's connected world. What is online privacy? Can you recall instances of personal information about yourself or others that you have seen on the Internet that in your opinion shouldn't be there? Have you ever seen, heard, or read something online that made you change your opinion of someone?

UPFRONT VOCABULARY

proactive	controlling a situation by making things happen rather than waiting for things to happen and then reacting to them*
candidate	a person who is trying to be elected or is applying for a job*

credentials	the qualities, training, or experience that make you suitable to do sth*
headhunter	a person whose job is to find people with the necessary skills to work for a particular company*
expertise	expert knowledge or skill in a particular subject, activity, or job*

*Definition courtesy of *Oxford Advanced Learner's Dictionary.*

👥 PRE-LISTENING VOCABULARY

Use a dictionary as necessary and work with your partner to fill in each blank with the most appropriate of these verbs from the listening. Adjust the verb tense and person as necessary.

embark   reject   enhance   span   nurture   portray

1. Professor Tilley's teaching career ____**spanned**____ three countries and 30 years.

2. In the film, Adriana _____ an elusive but charming industrial spy.

3. His thesis proposal was _____ because of its lack of clear focus.

4. The police lab technologist was able to _____ the picture with the new software.

5. I look forward to _____ on a new career as soon as I graduate.

6. As a child, Sophie _____ the dream of becoming a hockey player.

Note-Taking

 **Track 97**

Living in an increasingly connected world can be both a blessing and a curse. Information that we share online can instantly be seen around the world by the people we intend to share it with as well as anyone else, including marketing companies or prospective employers, who might be searching for information about you.

Any content such as pictures, videos, or opinions that you or your friends upload to the Internet that can be connected back to you is part of your social media footprint. You will listen to an interview with Linda Cicuta entitled "Social Networking and Your Electronic Footprint" that will help you consider carefully what you post online in order to not let your social media footprint get you into trouble.

Listen to the interview "Social Networking and Your Electronic Footprint" for the first time. As you listen, list the positives (pros) and negatives (cons) of keeping an online profile and write the strengths of each social networking tool as you hear them.

Positives of social networking:

- _____
- _____

Negatives of social networking:

- _____
- _____
- _____

List of strengths:

Blogs:

- _____
- _____

Twitter:

- _____
- _____

YouTube:

- _____

Facebook:

- _____
- _____

LinkedIn:

- _____
- _____

Listening STRATEGY

It is helpful for a listener to visualize what the speaker is describing—imagine a picture in the mind. As you listen try to envision or even draw a picture in your notes of what exactly this concept would look like.

Listening for the Main Ideas

Listen to the interview again, and answer the six questions by underlining the correct response.

 Track 98

1. Which is not one of the main ideas of the passage?
   a. increasing awareness of your online image
   b. investigating how to achieve the best salary and working conditions
   c. defining your electronic footprint and how it affects job search success

2. Who is this tutorial for?

   a. recent graduates who are going to start looking for work

   b. new university students who are looking for summer jobs

   c. both a and b

3. According to the listening, how do organizations use social media sites?

   a. to keep a close look on their employees

   b. for advertising and promotional purposes

   c. as a recruiting tool, for hiring

4. When Linda says you can "turn the tables around" she means

   a. Instead of companies looking at individuals, individuals can use social networking sites as part of the job search process.

   b. Instead of companies hiring based on resumés and CV, they can make these decisions by looking at online profiles.

   c. Instead of job searchers using traditional techniques to find jobs, they can use social media to promote their brand.

5. Which social networking site does Linda consider the most professional?

   a. Twitter

   b. LinkedIn

   c. Facebook

6. According to the audio, why should job seekers Google themselves?

   a. to see what one's future boss would see

   b. to see what one's own LinkedIn profile looks like

   c. to ensure that negative comments are not blown out of proportion

Listening Comprehension

 **Track 99**

Listen to the interview again, and for each group of sentences fill in the blanks by writing the provided words in the order they are used by the speaker. When you are finished, check your answers with your partner.

1. *recruiting tool, social profiles, electronic image, candidates*

   Eighty percent of companies use social networks as a _____. Sixty-six percent (of companies) said they had hired _____ using this method. Eighty percent review _____ before hiring. Seventy percent have rejected candidates because of their _____.

2. *impression, information, brand, imprint, footprint*

   Your online profile can make a big difference. It is your electronic _____, the impression or _____ you leave online, your trail of _____, your personal _____; what you do, say or portray online can leave an _____ on the viewer in either a positive or a negative way.

3. *recommendations, URL, key words, discussion, enquiries, boards*

Build a full profile; use _____ to get found by search engines; obtain a unique _____; include a photo; fill in the specialties section; get _____; join groups; connect with at least 50 members; follow companies; get on _____; keep it up to date; reply to requests and _____.

4. *honest, electronic, business, social, thorough*

Social Network: Ensure your online info is _____ and professional; take control of your _____ footprint; include a link to LinkedIn on your _____ card; set goals for using _____ media; decide how you will define your success; reply quickly to all queries and requests; be original and _____ — stand out; be proactive and reactive.

Personalizing

Linda suggests listing key words that will help search engines find your strengths, and then making a headline with those words. What are your key words? Find five or six job descriptions in your field or area of interest and paste them all into a website like wordcounter.net to find how often key words are used in a text. Write a headline using as many of them as you can and share it with the rest of your class.

Here is, for example, a list of key words that a website found for the job descriptions in Speaking Activity 5: work, media, skills, communication, social, and verbal.

An effective headline would be:

Highly Verbal Talent with Social Media and Communication Skills Available to Work for Your Company

My key words:

My headline:

Vocabulary and Language Chunks

Use a dictionary and the context of the sample sentences to help you understand these language chunks from the listening. Then, make your own sentences and share them with the class.

1. from the ground up

   I sold newspapers as a kid, and so learned about the industry from the ground up.

2. **blow out of proportion**

Shawn tends to exaggerate and blows these little incidents out of proportion.

_____

3. **provide outlets**

Writing provided the main outlet to his frustration.

_____

4. **on the flip side**

Vancouver weather is mild and is rarely cold. On the flip side, it rains a lot.

_____

5. **trail of information (information trail)**

The police used a trail of information, clues, and objects left by the suspect to track her down.

_____

6. **on the grapevine**

I've heard a rumour on the grapevine that class may be cancelled tomorrow.

_____

7. **electronic footprint**

By subscribing to many different social media sites, Steve created a large electronic footprint.

_____

SPEAKING 2

Communication Focus 3: Negotiating

Negotiation requires a series of strategies used to find a common ground or reach agreement between two parties. Bartering at a market for goods and settling on a price is one example where good negotiating skills are required. We negotiate all the time in all parts of our lives: with our family, with our friends, with our fellow students in group work.

Negotiation skills help us navigate successfully through work life in particular. Apply the following strategies when negotiating:

- Be interested in both the content of the negotiation and in the relationship with the other party.

- Realize that each side has interests based on basic human needs (security, recognition, autonomy).
- Find shared interests and focus on them. Separate the interests from the position.
- Communicate clearly, use appropriate emotion, and maintain a positive outlook.
- Listen actively and acknowledge what is being said.
- Put yourself in the other's shoes—try to see the situation as they see it.
- Increase options.
- Make your proposals consistent with the other side's values.
- Allow the other side to participate in the solving process.
- Build a working relationship; treat the negotiation as a side-by-side process.

SPEAKING ACTIVITY 12

Work together in groups of three and brainstorm to make a list of items that you can negotiate for or that you have negotiated for in the past. In your experience, can you negotiate for the same things in Canada as in your own country?

Example:

> cost and features of a cell phone plan

SPEAKING ACTIVITY 13

Imagine the following negotiations. In each case, list and discuss with your partner what you think each person's interests are.

Example:

> negotiation: You and employer   You want some time off.
>
> Employer interests: workflow, fairness, productivity . . .
>
> Your interests: family, health, responsibility . . .

Negotiation 1: You and teacher   You want a higher mark for this course.

Negotiation 2: You and landlord   You don't want to accept the landlord's rent increase.

Negotiation 3: You and auto dealer   You want a better price on a car you are considering.

SPEAKING ACTIVITY 14

Both columns of comments on the next page refer to the same situation. They are, however, from different perspectives because each person has different interests. Look at each line and discuss with your partner which issue is being addressed and who you sympathize with, the tenant or the landlord. Explain your choice.

Example:

> Tenant: The rent is already too high.
>
> Landlord: The rent hasn't been increased for a long time.
>
> Issue: cost, expenses
>
> Comment: I sympathize with the tenant because as a college student, I have fewer options and resources to deal with in a tight financial situation.

Tenant Perspective	Landlord Perspective
1. The rent is too high.	The rent hasn't been increased for a long time.
2. With other costs rising, I can't afford to pay more rent.	With other costs going up, I need more rental income.
3. The apartment needs painting.	The tenant has worn out the apartment.
4. I know people who pay less for a comparable apartment.	I know people who pay more for a comparable apartment.
5. Young people like me can't afford high rents.	Young people like this tenant tend to make noise.
6. The rent could be lower—the neighbourhood is run down.	We should raise rents to improve neighbourhood quality.
7. I am a desirable tenant with no dogs or cats.	This tenant's music drives me crazy.
8. I always pay the rent when the landlord asks for it.	This tenant doesn't pay the rent until I ask for it.
9. The landlord is unfriendly—never asks how things are.	I'm considerate; I never intrude on a tenant's privacy.

When you've finished, join another pair of your classmates, and start a new discussion about your own experiences when somebody else was in the same situation with you but perceived it differently.

ᴀ̂ᴀ̂ᴀ̂ SPEAKING ACTIVITY 15

Act out the following role play in small groups. Try to use negotiation strategies listed in Communication Focus 2. When you've finished, report your results to the class.

Group A. You are your company's supervisor in Toronto for a group of trainees from India. They have many complaints. You have not been told anything about their customs or religion. You find their English difficult to understand. They often get angry quickly and shout. You are talking to their leaders to find out what their problems are.

Try to reach some agreement.

Group B. You are the representatives of a group of trainees from India in Toronto. Your crew is having many problems with the Canadian supervisors. You feel that the Canadian company does not respect your religion.

a. Your team members are from the Malat religion. You cannot eat meat and you cannot sit at a table where meat is being eaten. The dormitory cafeteria has meat every day.

b. Your religion says you must pray outside every day at 5:00 PM. The schedule does not allow for this.

c. You must wear a turban at all times. A helmet (required by the company) will not fit over a turban.

d. Thursdays are a religious holiday. The company has a heavy training schedule on Thursdays.

Meet the Canadian representatives. Explain the problems.

Try to reach an agreement on all issues.

👥 SPEAKING ACTIVITY 16

Act out the following role-play with your partner. Try to use negotiation strategies listed above.

Person A. Your car was in a collision and the damage was so great it has been written off. You are negotiating the claim with the insurance company. Here are the details of your old car: 2010 Mazda 626; original price: $22,000; mileage: 40,000 km; features: AC, MP3/CD player, sunroof, Villeneuve driving seat, radial tires, fog lights.

Try to get as much as you can for your car.

Person B. You are an insurance claims adjuster. You must negotiate a claim with a client whose car has been written off in an accident. You base your evaluation on a similar car you found in a used car parking lot.

Features of similar car: 2009 Mazda 626; black book price (officially recognized Canadian car values): $8,000; mileage: 80,000 km; features: FM radio and cassette player.

Try to pay out as little insurance money as possible.

👥 SPEAKING ACTIVITY 17

Act out the following role play in small groups. Try to use negotiation strategies listed above. When you've finished, report your results to the class.

Group A. You wish to build a new luxury hotel in a small fishing village on the coast. You hope to develop the area as a swimming, yachting, and fishing resort. However, the local people are against your idea. Meet with the group of people from the village and find out what they want. After you have heard their grievances and needs, take a break to brainstorm with your partner(s) to think of ideas to give mutual benefits. Then, meet again with the villagers and try to persuade them to agree with your plan.

Group B. You are a group of residents from a small fishing village. A hotel group wishes to build a hotel in your village. You are against the plan for the following reasons:

- You are afraid of big changes in your way of life.
- You feel that many traffic problems will result.
- You feel that land prices and taxes will go up.
- You are afraid that too many trees and other greenery will be destroyed.
- other (Your group can brainstorm a reason.)

After you've met with the hotel group and told them your concerns, take a break to brainstorm for conditions under which you could accept the hotel group's plan.

PRONUNCIATION

Pronunciation Focus 1:
Projecting and Speaking Clearly

Misunderstandings often occur when speakers mumble or let their voices fade away. Good speakers will project their voice toward the audience (and even to the back row of the audience) rather than merely talking to the space immediately in front of them. Often the key to speaking more clearly is as easy as opening the mouth wider, or simply making a conscious decision that clarity is important and being aware of that while talking.

In the following activities you will practise six projection techniques: warm up, project the voice, vary loudness, find a comfortable pitch, add warmth to your expression, and enunciate.

 PRONUNCIATION ACTIVITY 1

Warm up before you start speaking. (Have water ready.)

Step 1. Speak from the diaphragm: stand up, hold your chest high, and laugh out loud:

Ha ha ha ha!!

Step 2. Breathe in deeply and quickly, exhale completely. Repeat.

Step 3. Exercise your jaw and lips: repeat these word groups:

toe toe toe toe toe toe

tie tie tie tie tie tie

two two two two two two

tea tea tea tea tea tea tea

may pay may pay may pay

mow bow mow bow mow bow

be me be me be me

flee flee flee flee flee flee

flow flow flow flow flow flow

we would we would we would

Step 4. Take a sip of your water.

Step 5. Repeat Steps 1–4.

Step 6. Relate an impromptu personal bio (two or three minutes of key achievements) to your partner.

PRONUNCIATION ACTIVITY 2

Project your voice.

Separate yourself from your partner by three or four metres and whisper messages to each other. Continue to move apart and whisper messages to each other. Speak from the diaphragm, pushing the sounds out and see how far apart you can get and still hear.

PRONUNCIATION ACTIVITY 3

Listen to the example sentences and note how they **vary loudness**. Then practise speaking the same sentences aloud and focus on varying the loudness like the speaker does.

 **Track 100**

Note: size of text relates to loudness (volume). The bigger the text, the louder the volume.

1. I ate an **or**ange not a **pea**ch

   1 2 3 **4** 5 6 7 **8**

2. a **boy**, a **girl**, a **house**, a **car**

   1 **2** 3 4 5 **6** 7 **8**

3. I just **don't know!** What did **I say?**

   1 2 3 4 5 6 7 8

PRONUNCIATION ACTIVITY 4

Find a comfortable pitch.

 **Track 101**

In music, the ranges of voice pitch are classified highest to lowest.

A. Listen to the audio recording of the example sentence in the various pitches.

soprano (highest)	"I landed my dream job."
alto	"I landed my dream job."
tenor	"I landed my dream job."
baritone	"I landed my dream job."
bass (lowest)	"I landed my dream job."

B. Read each of the following sentences out loud to your partner descending from highest to lowest pitch. Find the pitch in which you feel most comfortable and relaxed.

These pretzels are making me thirsty.

Canada Dry ginger ale is not too sweet.

 PRONUNCIATION ACTIVITY 5

Add warmth, personality, drama, and a smile to your expression. (Yes, you can hear a smile!) Practise reading the following sentences and adding a personal feeling to them.

I really love . . .

Hi, you've reached the home of _____. I'll be happy to call you back if you leave a message at the tone.

It's too bad you're out; I really wanted to wish you a happy birthday!

I'm so glad you are back; I missed you so much.

Hey! You said your dog doesn't bite.

 PRONUNCIATION ACTIVITY 6

Enunciate.

Using all the techniques you have used in the previous activities, record a voice message for your home phone. As you practise, before you record, use a mirror to confirm your jaw, lips, and tongue are moving.

Pronunciation Focus 2: Pausing for Effect

Good speakers pause between thought groups, at commas, and at periods to control the pace of their speech. Pausing can enhance the understanding of what you are saying and capture the audience's attention. It is a good practice to read out loud and to emulate (copy) professional speakers.

 PRONUNCIATION ACTIVITY 7

 **Track 102**

Listen to the reading of the text, paying attention to the placement and length of the pauses. Then practise reading the text out loud yourself.

I stumbled upon an interesting anecdote, called "Woman exemplifies good citizenship." In the story, a resident of Calgary made an ethical decision after finding a purse. A woman who acknowledged that she is homeless, and could certainly benefit from the $10,400 cash she found in the purse, decided to turn it in to authorities. She didn't expect a reward but would accept one, as long as she wouldn't have to reveal her identity, as the burden of family and friends knowing that she is homeless would be too embarrassing. When interviewed, she pointed out that she never considered keeping the money because of the criticism she would face from her peers. She also considers her actions as typical. She stated "most people would do the same."

PRONUNCIATION ACTIVITY 8

 **Track 103**

A. Listen to the use of pauses for emphasis in the following brief mini-speech. Often you can plan this kind of pause before or after a transition word, or before or after a key word.

Some years ago, Canadians said that the streets of Toronto were paved with gold, and the youth of Canada made their way there to find work, *[pause]* but *[pause]* today, there is a new job seeker hub . . .

The key to finding a job is, as it always has been, *[pause]* preparation *[pause]*: getting ready, and getting out there.

B. Write and practise making a mini-speech about a topic of your choice. Reflect on the transition words and key words in your speech and while practising, exaggerate your pauses. Record your speech, listen to yourself, and reflect on the effectiveness of your pausing.

COMMUNICATING IN THE REAL WORLD

Prepare a five-minute persuasive speech about a controversial topic. Start off by introducing yourself with a brief profile, then, using the persuasive language and pronunciation points in this chapter, try to convince your audience to change either their thinking or their actions on your topic by applying language functions from previous chapters as well as this one. For example, you may include a thorough analysis (Chapter 2) in your speech and support your proposition as you learned in Chapter 3. You may also want to use obligation phrases (Chapter 4), anecdotes (Chapter 5), and rhetorical expressions (Chapter 6) to appeal to your listeners' own personal interests.

Sample topics:

overuse of first language in ESL classes

English as an international language

cell-phone etiquette

cyber-bullying

SELF-EVALUATION

Think about your work in this chapter. For each row in the chart sections **Grammar and Language Functions**, **Pronunciation**, **Learning Strategies**, and **Note-Taking**, give yourself a score based on the rating scale below and write a comment in the Notes section.

Show the chart to your teacher. Talk about what you need to do to make your English better.

Rating Scale

1	2	3	4	5

Needs ⟵―――――――――――――――⟶ *Great!*
improvement.

	Score	Notes
Grammar and Language Functions		
preparing for a job interview		
arguing persuasively		
applying the passive voice		
negotiating		
Pronunciation		
projecting and speaking clearly		
pausing for effect		
Learning Strategies		
Speaking		
promoting yourself		
speaking persuasively		
Listening		
recognizing lists of examples or steps buried in a speaker's speech		
visualizing what the speaker is saying		
Note-Taking		
organizing by contrasting		
organizing by pros and cons		

Vocabulary and Language Chunks

Look at this list of new vocabulary and language chunks you learned in this chapter. Give yourself a score based on the rating scale and write a comment.

entrepreneur	founded	paint an accurate picture of	from the ground up
milestone	proactive	have a 9-to-5 job	blow out of proportion
hackathon	candidate	paint with broad strokes	provide outlets for
per se	credentials	cheat the system	on the flip side
freelancer	headhunter	stay on top of things	trail of information
relevant	expertise	have a sense of community	on the grapevine
broad	embark	come to the realization	electronic footprint
work history	reject	go above and beyond	
profile	enhance	avoid at all costs	
elusive	span	do more damage than good	
sector	nurture		
declare	portray		

	Score	Notes
understanding new vocabulary and language chunks		
using new lexical items freely and confidently		

My plan for practising is _____

_____

_____

_____

CREDITS

Photo and Figure Credits